Making Money in Brazil

Brazil Business Guide and Contacts

By Patrick W. Nee

The Internationalist®

www.internationalist.com

The Internationalist®

International Business, Investment, and Travel

Published by:
The Internationalist Publishing Company
96 Walter Street/Suite 200
Boston MA 02131, USA
Tel: 617-354-7722
www.internationalist.com
PN@internationalist.com

Welcome to the **Internationalist Business Guides** series:

The key to a successful business is knowing the markets. MAKING MONEY IN BRAZIL BRAZIL BUSINESS GUIDE AND CONTACTS offers executives, investors, and entrepreneurs the need-to-know information about doing business in Brazil.

Written as an in-depth, straightforward reference guide, this book lists key information about the Brazilian market, its challenges, and opportunities. It then looks into a dozen of Brazil's leading industries, their backgrounds, current situation, and projected course.

Whether you are looking to break into international business or need to update your knowledge on Brazilian markets— this comprehensive guide is for you.

The Internationalist

Contents

Chapter 1: Market Overview

The Federal Republic of Brazil is Latin America's biggest economy and is the fifth largest country in the world in terms of land mass and population with about 193 million people. It is the 7th largest economy in the world. Bolstered by strong domestic demand and a growing middle class, Brazil weathered the economic downturn better than most major economies and grew 7.5% last year, compared to an estimated 2.3% growth in the G7 countries and 2.8% in the United States. During the past decade, the country maintained sound macroeconomic policies to control inflation without sacrificing economic growth. This kept the inflation rate at 5.9% in 2010, and unemployment at 7.1%. Interest rates, though high compared to the rest of the world, remained historically low at the Central Bank rate of 10.75%. In 2010, the U.S. was Brazil's largest import supplier followed by China, Argentina, Germany, and South Korea.

The year 2010 ended with the U.S. holding a positive trade balance with U.S. merchandise exports to Brazil at US$ 35 billion, and imports from Brazil at US$ 24 billion. In 2010, Fitch gave Brazil an investment-grade rating which brought it in line with rankings from Standard & Poor's and Moody's Investors Service. In 2010, foreign reserves hit a record level at US$ 287.8 billion. Brazil's currency, the real, rose 34% against the dollar during the year.

Market Challenges

Brazil has a large and diversified economy that offers U.S. companies many opportunities to export their goods and services, and U.S. exports are increasing rapidly. That said, and despite noteworthy signs of improvements, there are a number of challenges in the Brazilian market, including uneven income distribution, poor public education, significant imbalance of market concentration, and an informal economy that hinders tax collection and keeps economic growth from reaching its full potential. These factors create a complex business environment with obstacles for U.S. exporters. Doing business in Brazil requires intimate knowledge of the local environment, including both the explicit as well as implicit costs of doing business (referred to as the "Custo Brasil").

Such costs are often related to distribution, government procedures, employee benefits, environmental laws, and a complex tax structure. Logistics pose a particular challenge, given the fragmented nature of distribution channels. Besides facing tariff barriers, U.S.
companies will find a complex customs system, and an overloaded legal system with a lengthy process for enforcing IPR and commercial law. Heavy taxes increase consumer prices up to 100%, while bureaucratic procedures and onerous product licensing also raise costs. The World Bank ranks Brazil 127 out of 183 economies in the world in terms of ease of doing business.

Market Opportunities

There are few, if any, sectors in Brazil that do not have excellent short term opportunities. Certain sectors of the Brazilian market have experienced higher than average growth, such as air transportation, telecom, oil and gas, and mining. Brazil will spend billions in infrastructure development of its roads, railroads, ports, and airports as well as in stadiums as it prepares for the World Cup in 2014 and the Olympics in 2016. Other promising areas for U.S. exports and investment include the following: agriculture, agricultural equipment, building and construction, electrical power, safety and security devices, environmental technologies, nuclear power, retail and transportation.

The Brazilian national oil company Petrobras' expansion may represent the largest global business opportunity in the oil & gas sector between the years 2011-20. The offshore pre-salt oil deposits discovered in 2006 and 2007 are estimated to exceed 60 billion barrels in probable or recoverable reserves, and could place Brazil among the world's top ten oil-producing countries. Petrobras anticipates that it will invest $224 billion in exploration and development between 2011 and 2015.

Brazil is targeting nuclear energy as an area for expansion in order to diversify its energy matrix and keep up with increased demand in a growing economy. The The Brazilian government intends to open a competitive bidding process in mid-to-late 2011 to construct four 1000MV nuclear reactors. This area offers substantial opportunity for government cooperation and commercial sales for U.S. companies.

Brazil is one of the largest IT markets within the emerging economies. IT end-user spending in Brazil is expected to grow to $134 billion in 2014. The largest share of spending will be on telecom equipment, representing 72% of the market, followed by IT services at 13.3%, and computing hardware at 11.9%.

In the years leading up to the 2016 Olympic Games in Rio de Janeiro, Brazil will host several international sporting events, including the 2011 World Military Games, the 2011-2012 Pan-American Maccabi Games, the 2013 soccer Confederations Cup, and the 2014 soccer World Cup. The Government of Brazil expects to invest $106 billion in the preparations for these events. These investments, which will include outlays for infrastructure, construction, transportation systems, port improvements, public security, and airport infrastructure upgrades, will present significant commercial opportunities for U.S. companies. Most of the major infrastructure upgrades will be carried out through Public-Private Partnerships under Brazil's Growth Acceleration Program.

Market Entry Strategy

Brazil's business culture is largely based upon personal relationships. Companies will need a strong presence and must invest time in developing relationships in Brazil. The U.S. Commercial Service encourages U.S. companies to visit Brazil to meet one-on-one with potential partners. One of the best ways to enter the Brazilian market is by attending a local trade show or using the U.S. Commercial Service's Gold Key Service (GKS). The U.S. Commercial Service can provide business counseling or arrange meetings with potential buyers through a GKS or during a trade show. U.S. companies have found it essential to work through a qualified agent or distributor when entering the Brazilian market. Some firms establish an office or joint venture in Brazil. Further discussion of these alternatives can be found in the

"Marketing Products & Services" chapter. It is extremely difficult for U.S. companies to get involved in public sector procurement without a local Brazilian partner.

Chapter 2: Selling U.S. Products and Services

Using an Agent or Distributor

Although some companies import directly from foreign manufacturers without local representation, in most cases the presence of a local agent or distributor can be very helpful. As in other countries, the selection of an agent requires careful consideration. Because of regional economic disparities, varying states of infrastructure, and a host of other issues, it is often difficult to find one distributor that has complete national coverage.

Lawyers recommend that exporters and representatives have a written agreement to help exporters limit liability for product defects, protect a trademark, better ensure payments, and define warranty terms. Clauses related to exclusivity and performance targets may be included within the agreement. The U.S. Commercial Service strongly suggests that U.S. companies consult with a Brazilian law firm before signing any agreement to avoid potential legal problems.

Establishing an Office

Either setting up a company in Brazil or acquiring an existing entity is an investment option in Brazil. Setting up new companies is relatively complex, although the Ministry of Development and International Trade (MDIC) has signaled a desire to simplify the process. According to the Ministry, the authorities have significantly reduced the amount of time required to grant various licenses and registrations over the past few years.

The Central Bank monitors acquisitions of existing companies. Corporations ("sociedades anonimas") and limited liability companies ("limitadas") are relatively easy to form. Local law requires that foreign capital be registered with the Central Bank. Failure to comply may cause serious foreign exchange losses, as well as problems with capital repatriation or profit remittance.

Franchising

Franchises account for approximately 25% of gross revenue in the retail sector. Local

Brazilian franchises dominate 90% of the market; however, foreign groups, particularly from the United States, are making headway. To take advantage of Brazil's growing market, U.S. franchisers will find it helpful to localize their products or services, invest in market research, and test market receptivity through pilot programs.

Brazil's Franchising Law states that franchisers or their master-franchisees should provide all potential franchisees with a Franchise Offering Circular (Circular de Oferta de Franquia). This must contain basic information about the financial health of the franchiser, as well as information on any pending legal disputes.

Direct Marketing
According to Acton International, a U.S.-based international direct marketing services provider, the Brazilian consumer receives an estimated 9.3 pieces of direct mail every month. Their research has shown that 74% of Brazilian consumers prefer receiving direct mail. With increased expendable income in the growing middle class, direct marketing is an effective

option to include in a company's marketing communications strategy for Brazil.

Brazil continues to lead Latin America in direct marketing activities due to its reliable postal service, large consumer base, and growing economy. The Brazilian Association of Direct Marketing (ABEMD) is a self- regulated, non-profit entity representing the direct marketing sector. Its web site provides important information regarding code of conduct, legislation compliance, and direct marketing service providers.

Joint Ventures/Licensing

Joint ventures are very common in Brazil, particularly as a way for foreign firms to compete for government contracts or in heavily regulated industry sectors, such as telecommunications and energy. Usually joint ventures are established through "sociedades anônimas" or "limitadas," which are similar to corporations and limited partnerships respectively. Licensing agreements are also common in Brazil.

The U.S. Commercial Service strongly advises hiring a competent local attorney with expertise in structuring such arrangements. (CS Brazil can facilitate this process through our Gold Key Service (click for more info). All licensing and technical assistance agreements, including trademark licenses, must be registered with the Brazilian Industrial Property Institute.

Selling to the Government

The Federal Government is Brazil's biggest buyer of goods and services. Winning contracts with the Brazilian Government can be challenging. U.S. exporters may find themselves at a competitive disadvantage without a significant in-country presence, as well as the patience and financial resources to respond to legal challenges and bureaucratic delays.

Brazilian Government procurement policies apply to purchases by government entities and parastatal companies. Government procurement regulations contained in Law 8666 establish an open competitive process for major government procurements. Under this law, price is the overriding factor in selecting suppliers. Tenders are open for international competition, either through direct bidding, consortia or imports; however, for many of the larger tenders (e.g. military purchases) single source procurements are possible if they meet the national interest or unique technical requirements. In case of a bid tie, nationally owned companies will gain preference over foreign competitors. More recent measures are focused on modernizing the tender process.

The Brazilian Constitution requires that all government purchases, whether at the federal, state or municipal levels, be contracted through public tenders. This process is regulated by the Brazilian Bid Law (Law # 8666, introduced in 1993). This law requires any and all official bidders to have a legal presence in Brazil. Law 8666 establishes general requirements for tenders and administrative contracts for goods and services at the Federal, State, and Municipal levels.

On December 16, 2010, Brazil published a decree (often referred to as the "Buy Brazil Act") that provides preferential treatment for domestic suppliers over foreign firms even if the Brazilian company's prices are up to 25% higher. Brazil is not a signatory to the WTO Government Procurement Agreement, which precludes discrimination against goods and services from other signatory countries. The preference applies to government procurement at all levels, including federal, state and local, although there has been discussion about allowing exemptions specifically for Games-related security items. As a result, U.S. companies may find it difficult to participate in Brazil's public sector procurement unless they are associated with a local firm. Government procurement of foreign telecommunications and information technology equipment is exempt from the above requirements. Special requirements were established in 1993 and 1994 allowing locally manufactured telecommunications and IT products to receive preferential treatment in government procurement, and to be eligible for tax incentives and other fiscal benefits based on local content and other requirements.

It is often difficult for foreign companies to sell to Brazil's public sector unless they are associated with a local firm. To be considered a local firm, a firm must have a majority of Brazilian capital participation and decision-making authority, or operational control. A Brazilian state enterprise is permitted to subcontract services to a foreign firm if domestic expertise is unavailable, while a foreign firm may only bid to provide technical services when there are no qualified Brazilian firms.

In the case of international tenders to supply goods and services for government projects, successful bidders are required to have local representation -- i.e., a legal presence in Brazil. Since the open period for bidding is often as short as one month, it is advisable to have a resident partner in Brazil.

Including Brazilian goods and services in your company's bid, or significant subcontracting association with a Brazilian firm, may improve your company's chance for success. Similarly, a financing proposal that includes credit for the purchase of local goods and services for the project will be more attractive. Advance descriptions of U.S. suppliers' capabilities can prove influential in winning a contract, even when they are provided before the exact terms of an investment plan are defined or the project's specifications are completed. Such a proposal should include financing, engineering, and equipment presentations.

Distribution and Sales Channels

All of the customary import channels exist in Brazil: agents, distributors, import houses, trading companies, subsidiaries and branches of foreign firms, among others. Brazilian importers generally do not maintain inventory of capital equipment, spare parts, or raw materials, partly because of high import and storage costs. Recently, because of the creation of additional bonded warehouses, industries that rely heavily on imported components and parts are maintaining larger inventories in these warehouses.

Selling Factors/Techniques

Price and payment terms are extremely important sales factors. Generally, U.S. goods are perceived as high quality; however, depending on quality as the primary competitive advantage may be risky as the opening of the Brazilian market in the early 1990s brought greater foreign and domestic competition. To be competitive, U.S. companies should adapt their products to local technical requirements and culture. Competing with an ever increasing amount of Chinese imports can be difficult because of their lower price; therefore, emphasizing product quality, customer service, and warranty terms are key factors for U.S. companies.

Electronic Commerce

As Latin America's most advanced internet and e-commerce market, Brazil offers additional marketing and business opportunities. Brazil is the fifth largest Internet market in the world and the largest in Latin America. Determining factors for the development of e-commerce include the increase in broadband penetration and per capita income, improvement in cyber security, and a higher number of credit card holders. Beyond the social and infrastructure considerations, the fact that the region has a large portion of its population between 18 and 35 years old significantly influenced the results of B2C (business to consumer) e-commerce. In light of Brazil's continued economic expansion, lowered taxes on personal computers, and the government's pledge to extend internet access to all its citizens, there is plenty of room for growth for e-commerce in this market.

Trade Promotion and Advertising

With its well-established and diversified industrial sector, Brazil has a variety of specialized publications that can provide excellent advertising outlets. TV advertising can also be an important marketing channel for Brazil's growing consumer base. The top advertising categories by expenditure are trade and commerce, consumer services, culture, leisure, sports and tourism, media, as well as public and social services.

The most popular magazine in Brazil, with a circulation of over one million copies, is the weekly Veja, published by the Abril Publishing Company. The largest daily circulation newspaper is Folha de São Paulo, published by the Folha Group, with a circulation of 400,000

on Sundays and a daily circulation of 317,000 from
Monday through Saturday.

Participating in trade fairs is another important marketing tool. The city of São Paulo hosts around 300 trade fairs per year, and other cities host significant shows as well, e.g. for oil and gas (Rio de Janeiro) and for mining (Belo Horizonte). These events attract many visitors and exhibitors from Brazil and foreign countries. Specialists from the U.S. Commercial Service Brazil participate in many of these events, and can help you arrange meetings with potential agents, distributors, lawyers, and customers at these trade shows.

Pricing

Payment terms are extremely important in Brazil because of the country's high interest rates. In fact, it is not unusual for a local company to select a U.S. supplier with higher prices but better finance terms. In Brazil, all import-related costs are generally high because of import duties and taxes – thus some U.S. companies implement efficient logistics systems and lower profit margins. In some cases costs are so high that a simple calculation may indicate that your margins will not allow you to compete with a local product.

Sales Service/Customer Support

The "Consumer Protection Law" of 1992 requires customer support and after-sales servicing. In the case of imported products, the importer or the distributor is responsible for such services; therefore, U.S. manufacturers should appoint agents or distributors who are qualified to provide such services.

Protecting Your Intellectual Property

Several general principles are important for effective management of intellectual property rights (IPR) in Brazil. First, it is important to have an overall strategy to protect your company's IPR. Second, IPR is protected differently in Brazil than in the United States. Third, rights must be registered and enforced in Brazil, under local laws.

Companies may wish to seek advice from local attorneys or IPR consultants. The U.S.

Commercial Service can provide a list of local lawyers upon request. Intellectual property is primarily a private right, and the U.S. government generally cannot enforce rights for private individuals. In Brazil, it is the responsibility of the owners of these rights to register, protect, and enforce them where relevant by retaining their own counsel and advisors. While the U.S. Government is willing to assist, there is little we can do if the rights holders have not taken the fundamental steps necessary to secure and enforce their IPR in a timely fashion. Moreover, in many countries, intellectual property rights' holders, who delay enforcing their rights due to the mistaken belief that the USG can provide a political resolution to a legal problem, may find that their rights have been abrogated due to doctrines such as statutes of limitations, laches, estoppel, or unreasonable delay in prosecuting a law suit. In no instance should USG advice be seen as a substitute for the obligation of a rights' holder to promptly pursue their case.

It is always advisable to conduct due diligence on your local partners. Keep the interests of your partner in mind and give your partner clear incentives to honor their contract with you. A good partner is an important ally in protecting IPR. Keep an eye on your cost structure. Projects and sales in Brazil require constant attention, so you should work with legal counsel familiar with Brazilian laws to create a solid contract that includes non- compete clauses, as well as confidentiality and non-disclosure provisions. It is also recommended that small- and medium-size companies understand the importance of working together with trade associations and organizations to support efforts to protect IPR and stop counterfeiting. There are a number of these organizations, both Brazil and U.S.-based. These include:

The U.S. Chamber and local American Chambers of Commerce

National Association of Manufacturers (NAM)

International Intellectual Property Alliance (IIPA)

International Trademark Association (INTA)

The Coalition Against Counterfeiting and Piracy

International Anti-Counterfeiting Coalition (IACC)

Pharmaceutical Research and Manufacturers of
America (PhRMA)
Biotechnology Industry Organization (BIO)
National Institute of Industrial Property (INPI -
Brazil)

The IPR Climate in Brazil

Although Brazil ratified the Agreement on
Trade-Related Aspects of Intellectual Property
Rights – TRIPS, Brazilian law regarding
intellectual property incorporates international
standards in effect since 1996. The most relevant
IPR agency in Brazil is the National Institute of
Industrial Property - INPI - which has been an
active participant in international fora seeking to
amplify the concept of intellectual property and
remain up- to-date with the international
community. This posture reflects Brazil's
significant improvement on copyright
enforcement, according to the USTR Special
301 report regarding intellectual property
protection. INPI is also taking measures to
increase Brazil's patent processing capacity by
hiring specialists, raising salaries and
modernizing equipment. Brazil has also ratified
the World Intellectual Property Organization

Treaties on Copyright, Performances and Phonograms.

Due Diligence

In Brazil, the U.S. Commercial Service (USCS) can provide U.S. companies with lists of well-known and respected credit rating companies and law firms that can conduct credit checks on potential customers or provide important legal advice. Additionally, the USCS Brazil offers U.S. companies detailed background information, including visits to the target company, through its International Company Profile (ICP).

Chapter 3: Leading Sectors for U.S. Export and Investment

Overview

Brazil has thirteen industrial production facilities owned by seven large agricultural equipment manufacturers. Most of the international agricultural machinery producers are manufacturing locally and exporting agricultural machinery to other South American countries. These companies include Agco, Agrale, Caterpillar, John Deere, Komatsu, Valtra and CNH (Case, Fiat Allis and New Holland). Total installed production capacity in Brazil is 86,000 machines per year.

A large portion of the agricultural machinery manufactured in Brazil is for exports, with South American countries representing over 56% of Brazilian exports of agricultural machinery. Exports of tillers, wheel tractors, crawler tractors, combines, loaders and backhoes, where seriously affected by the devaluation of the Dollar in face of the Real, and 2010 exports decreased 51% when compared to 2009.

Best Prospects/Services

Top U.S. export prospects in this sector include sophisticated, state-of-the-art machinery with higher efficiency levels, including the following equipment: post-harvest machinery, including field refrigeration units/storage for tropical fruits; fruit, grain, seed and vegetable cleaning, sorting and grading machinery; GPS and precision agriculture devices; and poultry equipment.

Opportunities

Brazil is a major producer of a variety of agricultural commodities and is the world's largest producer of coffee, sugarcane and oranges. It is also the world's second largest producer of soybeans, cattle meat, poultry, tobacco leaves, bananas and brazil nuts, and the third largest producer of maize, pineapples, pepper, and cashew nuts. Besides already being an agriculture powerhouse, Brazil is also one of the few countries still capable of increasing its planted area. In fact, Brazil has more unused commercially viable agricultural land than any other country in the world.

This strength in the agricultural sector means there is growing demand for agricultural equipment that improves the quality and yield of crops and reduces costs. Moreover, since farms are generally large, Brazil is ideally suited to incorporate a wide range of American agricultural machinery and technology.

Brazilian farmers enjoy a comparative advantage in many agricultural segments, particularly the grain, fruit, fiber, and animal protein sectors. This advantage is due to a temperate climate with plenty of light, the world's largest surface and ground fresh water reserves, excellent quality and diversity of soils and diverse agro-ecological systems.

Brazil is ranked as the fifth largest aviation market in the world with more than 190 million potential passengers. The tremendous increase in the demand for this sector is driven by the country's economic growth. The market will continue to expand to receive visitors for the 2014 World Cup and Olympic Games in 2016.

Best Products and Services

The Brazilian aircraft manufacturing company, Embraer, ended 2010 with a solid performance, delivering 69 jets to the airlines and executive jet segments. Compared to the same period in the previous year, deliveries of executive jets more than doubled, from 19 to 40, while deliveries to airlines dropped from 35 to 29 aircraft. Brazil has the seventh largest helicopter fleet in the world, with approximately 1,255 helicopters. More than 42 % of this total is concentrated in the State of São Paulo. In 2011, the helicopter market is expected to continue to grow. For instance, demand within the state of São Paulo alone will lead to an increase of 22% in the helicopter fleet. The offshore oil segment presents most of the growth opportunities in this segment due to the enormous investments the Brazilian Government is making in the pre-salt oil- fields.

Opportunities
As Brazil's aviation market continues to expand, imports of parts and components will continue to increase, representing good business

opportunities for U.S. suppliers. The products expected to have the most potential are: airplane and helicopter parts and components for defense and executive aircraft. In the long term, the law enforcement segment should also present good business prospects as Brazil prepares for the World Cup in 2014 and the 2016 summer Olympic Games.

Airports

Between 2011 – 2014, the Brazilian Federal Government expects to invest approximately around US$ 3 billion to improve operation and installations of 14 airports located in the 12 host cities of the 2014 World Cup. Today, these 14 airports generate 87 percent of Brazilian air traffic.

The GoB is discussing a concession model with Brazilian development bank BNDES to incorporate private capital and management into enlarging its airports, initially targeting Guarulhos (Sao Paulo), Viracopos (Sao Paulo) and Brasilia, with Confins (Belo Horizonte) and Galeao (Rio de Janeiro) airports to follow. The GoB is conducting a feasibility study that will explore various options that include concessions, public-private partnerships (PPP) or PPP-based management of airport terminals. It plans to initiate a bidding process in November 2011, with the aim of selecting finalists in December 2011 or January 2012. There are plans to enlarge all other airports, but details are not yet available.

The first auction to create a Public-Private Partnership (PPP) for the renovation and expansion of the São Gonçalo do Amarante airport in Natal (RN) will be held July 19, 2011 at the BM&F / Bovespa in São Paulo. Bidding will begin June 19, 2011 and those interested in the concession will have until July 12, 2011 to deliver the necessary documentation. Passenger traffic at this airport is predicted to grow to approximately 4.9 million passengers in 16 years.

INFRAERO is the leading end user-user of airport and ground support equipment in Brazil. INFRAERO buys all of its equipment through government public bids that are published on its website 15- 30 days prior to their opening for competition: www.infraero.gov.br In any tender with INFRAERO, three factors influence the final decision: First, the company must properly submit all of the requested documentation. Second, the company and its products must meet INFRAERO's quality standards. Finally, once the first two criteria are met, INFRAERO then chooses the company offering the lowest cost. International companies are welcome to participate in the public bids. However, it is required that they have a local legal representative in Brazil.

Brazil's airport infrastructure upgrades present significant business opportunities for U.S. companies to provide products such as passenger bridges, baggage handling systems, handling equipment, check-in conveyors, x-ray integration, baggage claim carousels, X- ray machines and others safety and security equipment.

Information Technologies
Brazil is the second-largest information technology (IT) market within emerging economies after China. Brazil has the most-balanced IT market segments among BRIC

countries as determined by size, macroeconomic strength, growth, and the balance maintained between consumer and business IT spending. According to a report from Gartner last year, IT end-user spending in Brazil is expected to grow the next four years to $134.2 billion. This represents a compound annual growth rate (CAGR) of 7.3% from 2010 through 2014. The largest share of spending will be telecom in 2010, representing 72 % of the market and a five-year CAGR of 6.4%. This is followed by IT services (13.3%) and computing hardware (11.9%). In 2014, IT services are forecast to represent 15.4% of total IT spending, while telecom will drop to 69.9%. Investments in IT will continue to be strong due to the 2014 soccer World Cup and the 2016 summer Olympic Games. Infrastructure must be built and upgraded for both major events, but they will also require investments in tourism facilities, transportation and security which all will have an IT component.

Brazil is the 5th largest personal computer (PC) market in the world. It also drives Latin America's PC market with 41.5% share. In the long term, Brazil is forecast to continue experiencing the largest growth rates in this region until at least 2014. Brazil's trade policy has clearly favored domestic production of PCs over importation of complete assembled PCs. Tariffs for completed PCs are high as an incentive to add local content, and despite recent policy changes, the trend will likely continue, compelling foreign vendors to establish manufacturing and assembly facilities within Brazil. Government policy in Brazil also stipulates PC manufacturers need to maintain a minimum ratio of R&D investment to revenue. This ratio has been raised to 3%, from 2%, and effectively encourages domestic manufacturers to innovate and remain competitive vis-à-vis foreign products. In addition, consumers receive tax breaks for buying PCs. Consumer purchases of PCs costing less than R$4,000 (about US$2,275) are currently tax-exempt. The 9.25% PIS/COFINS tax exemption will continue to encourage PC consumption and advance PC literacy.

According to Gartner, Brazil's PC market is forecast to grow an average of 16.7% per year until 2014, with the bulk of growth centering on mobile PCs. This form factor will grow an average of 28% over the same period due to the relatively low current penetration rate, an increase in local production by Brazilian manufacturers, lower-cost application service providers (ASPs), more easily available credit, an increase in Brazilians' average income and more foreign direct investment. Desk-based PCs will grow 8.6% for similar reasons, as well as to meet demand from business replacement cycles.

Perspectives for 2011 are positive. The Brazilian Electric-Electronic Association believes that the industry will continue to grow faster than the country's GDP for 2011. The main reasons for growth in Brazil's IT hardware segment are economic stability, lower dollar values and tax exemption on computer sales through the "Lei do Bem." Though this law was targeted at the PC and notebook segment of the market, increased computer sales also results in increased demand for printers. According to industry forecasts, 2011 should be the "Year of the Tablets", as mobile computer sales will continue to grow, and retail experts predict that within two months of the launch of the lower-priced notebooks, prices could drop even lower because of increased sales volume for computer components and the expected weakness of the U.S. dollar, since many components are imported. Sales of corporate network servers in Brazil should increase this year. Falling prices for network equipment and the computerization of small and medium-sized companies are among the factors contributing to growth. Brazil will continue to import computer hardware and peripherals as local production cannot keep pace with demand, while PC manufacturers may not be able to meet demand because of some processor shortages.

Telecommunication Equipment and Services

Brazil remains Latin America's largest telecom market with more than 35% of the region's revenues. Services continue to drive the sector with total revenues of US$60 billion split among fixed carriers (28%), mobile carriers (38%), and general services (22%), while manufactured products account for US$ 7.9 billion (12%). Manufactured products experienced a 9% decrease as compared to previous year mainly due to the low exchange rate. Motorola, Nokia, Nortel and Cisco have manufacturing facilities in Brazil, giving the country one of the region's best telecom infrastructures.   Brazil's telecommunications sector has seen some drastic changes over the last two years, with the merger of mobile carriers Brasil Telecom and Oi, Vivendi (French Group) buying into GVT (Brazilian telecom carrier), the launch of the long-awaited national broadband plan, and most recently, Telefónica taking full control of Vivo. Brazil seems to be on a roll, having been virtually untouched by the 2008-09 global financial crises and abuzz with preparation for the World Cup in 2014 and the Olympics in 2016.

With a promising economic outlook and rising prosperity, demand for broadband in Brazil is expected to soar. Broadband operators have been struggling to keep up with the growing demand, which has led to problems of system overload. Brazil's government has been drawing up plans to spread broadband across the vast country in one of the world's largest infrastructure projects.

Two major factors have inhibited the growth of broadband in Brazil: shortage of fixed-line infrastructure, and broadband prices, which are too high for many Brazilians. On the other hand, the growth of mobile broadband in Brazil has been nothing short of spectacular, attracting more than four million subscribers.

Cellular Phone Services: The digital gap between Brazil and developed regions like Europe is closing, and Brazil will not be far behind its US and European counterparts in launching Long Term Evolution Technologies (LTE) expected for late 2012. The arrival of LTE will bring opportunities for equipment suppliers to provide new solutions that will leverage the main benefits of technology, spectral efficiency, improved signaling capacity and increased energy efficiency. Telecom operators recognize the need to broaden their offerings in order to win the loyalty of new customers, retain existing users, and benefit from the market potential of non-voice services. Price cutting and value- added services including: faster data transmission, enhanced multimedia capabilities and improved new types of media are the most critical strategies for luring customers. Satellites: After years of stagnation, the satellite market grew 9% in 2010. The demand for this service is still growing especially in the video segment, e-learning and broadband services in the remote areas of the country. Market analysts are witnessing strong growth in demand for backhaul - not only from telecom companies, but also from the financial services and retail segments - while there is also potential with government- driven universal access initiatives. New compression technologies will force the reduction of prices for this type of services and as a result of that, regional broadcasters are planning to change the current microwave distribution infrastructure for satellite solution. There are good prospects for trunking services for regions where there is no optical fiber, distant learning, corporate TV (with media and sales points), and municipalities that are interested in building its own Internet network.

Broadband: The Brazilian Government unveiled Brazil's national broadband plan (NBP) aimed at addressing Brazil's soaring broadband usage demand. The proposal, entitled "A national plan for broadband - Brazil at high speed," lays out the government's goals, to be accomplished by 2014 when Brazil hosts the World Cup, of increasing individual access to fixed broadband service in Brazil to 30 million people, providing 60 million users with mobile broadband access, and connecting all government agencies, public schools, public health facilities, public libraries, and federal state and local law enforcement agencies to the plan's expanded broadband network. The plan also calls for the construction of 100 thousand new community telecenters with broadband access designed to reach the rural areas of Brazil. The plan envisions a concession model that utilizes existing telephone fiber optic networks, and calls for government investment of U.S. $26 billion plus $49 billion in private investment.

Power Line Communications (PLC) –Anatel, the Brazilian equivalent to FCC, approved the regulation on Broadband Systems over Power Line. The document sets the permission for the use of this technology in the band between 1.705 kHz and 50MHz. Companies like AES

Eletropaulo Telecom and Copel are testing the technology to decide about investments to be made in order to provide these services. Pay TV Market: The Brazilian market for Pay TV generated gross revenue of US$5 billion as of September 2010 with approximately 9.1 million subscribers. This market is expected to grow at least 10% in the next year mainly because of the increase of the broadband penetration in country. Auction of 3.5 GHz WiMAX bands still on hold: Brazil's telecommunications regulatory agency, ANATEL, is planning to auction the 3.5 GHz frequency band in the first half of 2011. After public consultations the agency is still evaluating the best model to auction this frequency in order to increase competition between players and minimize the prices of services to customers. The main issue is whether fixed line operators can take part in the auction in regions where they already provide telephony services. In December 2010, Anatel auctioned the 1.9-2.1 gigahertz frequency band auction and Nextel Brazil was the winning bidder for 20-megahertz licenses and now has secured the rights to operate 3G systems in all regions of the country.

Opportunities for U.S. suppliers exist in the areas of 3G-network maintenance, Long Term Evolution (LTE) and WiMax services and applications, broadband internet infrastructure, application software, and wireless communication networks. Trends continue to be toward convergence, i.e., adding telecommunications services, to maximize the benefits derived from investments and efficient operations. Best prospects for US suppliers include all type of solutions to improve the broadband market via cable modem, home networking platforms, IP telephones, IPTV software and video-on- demand services, among others.

Transportation

The Brazilian transportation infrastructure faces many challenges. Roads and ports need to be upgraded. Trucks hauling cargo on roads are the most used method of transportation. Despite the existence of several rivers, waterways are rarely used. The exception is the Amazon region, where rivers are usually the only way of access to many isolated villages. Railroads are few and uncompetitive. The use of trains for long distance transportation of passengers is restricted to a few urban tourist routes, while cargo transportation is mostly restricted to minerals.

According to the National Logistics and Transport Plan (PNLT) established in April 2007, the investments needed to reduce bottlenecks in the transportation sector for the medium and long term reaches a total amount of US\$ 220 billion between 2008 and 2023. Investments include extension of highways; the interconnection of the North- South regions with Southeast; ferries to cover North-South regions; and port construction. Aware of the need to improve its transportation infrastructure in time for the 2014 World Cup, the Brazilian government has pledged billions of dollars to improve the urban transit system in the twelve host cities. To meet other needs, Brazil is developing new concessions and public-private partnerships, leveraging the private sector in a way that is mutually beneficial to investors and the government.

Waterways: Brazil's participation in the waterway modal of transportation is small when compared with other countries. For example, 25% of cargo is transported by river in the United States and 35% in Canada. In Brazil, only 13% of cargo is transported by this mode. Brazil has enormous potential for river traffic with approximately 63,000 km of rivers and lakes, of which 40,000 km are navigable. However, the potential is still largely untapped, with navigation occurring in only 13,000 km, with a greater concentration in the Amazon region. Lack of storage facilities, limited access and few terminals are the main problems faced by this segment. Currently the largest share of investments comes from the public sector, representing 97% of the funds (or about $ 3 billion per year). This situation is expected to change by the end of 2022, when mixed investments (private and public) may reach an average annual investment of $4.6 billion.

Ports: The low use of port services originates from old problems of infrastructure: (a) difficulties of access to ports by road and railways, (b) lack of strategic planning, causing cargo to pile up in ports, and (c) lack of investment in the existing ports. New investments are expected to be made in this segment to increase the participation of water transportation from current 14% to 29% in 2025. This growth will enable the reduction of tariffs and freight cost and contribute to reducing the flow of trucks on highways.

Railways: By 2015, the Brazilian federal government plans to invest US$40 billion in rail transportation, mainly expanding the network of 28,000 kilometers to 35,000 kilometers. Moreover, by 2023, investment in sector projects could reach US$73.4 billion. Compared to emerging countries, Brazil has less than half of China railroads and six times less than India.

The government's goal is to make the railways the main means of transporting freight in the country. Today, the roads represent 58% of the total freight while railroads comprise 21%. Transport by rail can be up to 30% cheaper and more efficient than paved roads. A freight car loads nearly ten times more than a truck. Logistics: Brazil has one of the highest logistics costs in the world. In 2010 the World Bank estimated that the distribution cost structure includes approximately 31.8% of logistics cost. This includes administration, warehousing, inventory, legal requirements and transportation costs. The same report shows that the logistics cost represent an average of 20% of the GDP (twice that of the United States).

World Cup 2014: Brazilian cities will have to invest heavily in the modernization and expansion of their transportation systems, and the World Cup is the incentive Brazil needs. Brazil plans to invest in the construction of new metro lines, the implementation of light rail vehicles (LRV) and Bus Rapid Transit (BRT), and other infrastructure projects to make its transportation system modern.

The current metrorail system in all Brazilian cities transports about 6 million people daily. That should be the number of people transported by the metro system in the metropolitan area of São Paulo alone. According to a study done by ANTP (National Association of Public Transportation), the social cost incurred by the city of São Paulo due to its current insufficient public transportation system is about US$ 22 billion a year. Furthermore, the study showed that 63% of the cities with more than 300 thousand people use illegal, unsafe and unreliable means of transportation with millions of people spending 3 to 6 hours a day traveling to and from work or school. While there are many problems in the current system, this also means there are a lot of opportunities for growth and investment, including for U.S. companies.

Privatization in the transportation sector increased over the last 20 years. Many antiquated and burdensome state management structures that operated in the sector have been dismantled. The Brazilian railroad industry has been privatized through concession contracts ranging from 30 to 60 years, and the ports sector is experiencing similar, albeit less expansive, privatization. In response to the dramatic deterioration in the national highway system, the federal government has granted concessions for existing highways to private companies, which in turn promise to restore, maintain, and expand these highways in exchange for toll revenues generated. Brazil has historically invested in other sectors to the detriment of infrastructure. Now, the country faces an infrastructure deficit. Recent growth and a net of opportunities arising in Brazil will be the thrust the country needed to shift its focus to the infrastructure. International and domestic pressure to host the World Cup in 2014 should compel Brazil to finally develop a modern transport infrastructure, generating high return on investment while providing development and benefits to the population. With the government creating new concessions and public-private partnerships, it has never been easier to entry Brazil's transportation market.

Import Costs: All imports in Brazil are subject to a number of taxes and fees, which are usually paid during the customs clearance process. There are four main taxes that account for the bulk of importing costs:

Import duty: is a federal tax levied on foreign products that enter Brazilian territory and is calculated on top of the CIF value. For the electronic security equipment, import duty ranges from 2 to 20 percent depending on the product. The average duty rate is 15 percent.

Industrial Products Tax (IPI): is a federal tax levied on both domestic and imported manufactured products. It is assessed at the point of sale by the manufacturer in the case of domestically produced products, but at the point of customs clearance in the case of imports. The IPI is calculated on top of the CIF value plus import duty. The IPI for electronic security equipment varies from 10 to 20 percent.

Merchandise Circulation Tax (ICMS): is a state government value-added tax, applicable to both imported and domestic products. The ICMS tax on imports is assessed over the CIF value, plus import duty, plus IPI as its calculation base. The calculation of this tax is done in a way that the ICMS tax is calculated on top of itself. The ICMS rate varies among states. In the state of São Paulo it is 18 percent, but in most states it is 12 percent.

PIS and Cofins: these fees are applicable to both domestic and imported products and services. They are calculated in an extremely complex way on top of themselves. In general, the total effect of these fees sums up to approximately 12.63 percent of the CIF.

Brazilian manufacturers must also pay the above taxes, but American companies should keep in mind that, as the taxes are calculated in a compounding manner over the CIF value plus the import duty, the overall IPI, ICMS, PIS and Cofins of an imported product will be significantly higher than that of a locally manufactured product. Also, when distributors and trading companies sell the product, they are compensated for those taxes collected at the time of import.

Electrical Power

thBrazil is the 10 largest power operator in the world. Brazil's electricity generation industry is largely in the hands of the Federal and State Governments. The Federally owned power company, Eletrobras, controls over 40 percent of Brazil's installed generation capacity; energy companies owned by various State Governments control approximately 35 percent; while the remaining 25 percent of generating capacity has been privatized. Brazil has 2,324 operational power projects with 111,496 megawatts (MW) or 111,496,618 kW of installed capacity (excluding imports).

Projecting an annual GDP growth rate of 5.1 percent, Brazil's electricity consumption is expected to jump from 455.2 terawatt-hour (TWh) in 2010 to 712 TWh in 2019, while the country's installed capacity is expected to reach 167,078 MW. Brazil's Power Research Company's (EPE) figures indicate that compared with December 2010, the share of capacity supplied by hydroelectricity should be reduced to 69.85 percent by December 2019. If all eight planned nuclear plants come online, natural gas power plants may also be reduced to about 7 percent, while nuclear generation may reach 2 percent. However, gas plants may be revamped again, if significant oil and gas sub-salt fields come on line over the next ten years.

Renewable Energy
Solar energy through photovoltaic technology (PV) is a competitive alternative to grid extension but is limited to remote areas of the country and to applications that promote social

interests such as electricity supply to schools, hospitals, water pumping systems, and other uses. Currently ANEEL data shows only three small PV plants in operation (3, 12 and 20 kW), with a fourth one being constructed by MPX Energia, which is authorized to generate 5 MW. National oil company Petrobras is also evaluating one new pilot PV project not to exceed 30 MW. There are several other small PV systems already installed, mainly by Universities, but they have not been registered with ANEEL. Estimates indicate that 5 to 10 percent of the homes without electricity could be supplied with PV water heating systems. However, the technology is considered costly and the required maintenance is sometimes complex. On the other hand, the use of solar water heaters in Brazil has increased rapidly in the past few years, with nearly 150 Brazilian manufacturers producing these products for residences, hotels, hospitals, and swimming pools.

The Brazilian government envisions wind power playing a greater, though still modest role, (about 3.6 percent), in Brazil's power matrix by

2019. Brazil's National Electric Energy Agency (ANEEL) held two wind power auctions in 2009 and 2010, where 3,850 megawatts (MW) were contracted with energy from 141 wind power plants scheduled to be delivered by 2013. Brazil currently has 48 operating wind power plants, nineteen under construction, and another 84 pending construction. In September 2010, ANEEL published a draft resolution to reduce the barriers for the installation of small-size renewable power generation connected to the power grid. The resolution is still open for public comments and includes solar, wind, biomass, and small hydropower plants.

The estimated 2011 market for Brazil's power generation, transmission, and distribution (GTD) equipment market is projected to be US$7.1 billion (**) of which US$545 million is projected to be imported with about US$ 70 million of that import total coming from the United States.   The participation of foreign equipment suppliers has increased over the past year and is projected to remain steady over the next years, if the Brazilian Real currency remains strong in relationship to the U.S. dollar.

ABINEE reports that the local industry is concerned, as foreign suppliers have been actively supplying equipment and services for important projects, such as the Rio Madeira power generation plant and the Tucurui-Manaus transmission line. EPE's 2010-2019 Power Expansion Plan calls for investments of US$99 billion to bring an additional 63,482 MW of power generation capacity into Brazil's power grid. Government-owned Eletrobras and its subsidiaries estimate that they invested US$3.4 billion in 2010. This figure includes investment by Eletrobras' private consortia partners. Increased power generation accounted for the bulk of the Eletrobras' investments of US$1.5 billion. From 2010 to 2014, Eletrobras and its subsidiaries plan to invest approximately US$25.4 billion.

This amount includes investment by its private sector partners as well as Eletrobras itself. A total of 39,740 MW of power has been contracted for delivery from 2010 to 2019 through Brazil's electrical power auctions, including the giant 11,000 MW Belo Monte hydro plant auctioned off in April 2010. Belo

Monte alone will call for approximately US$9.5 billion in investments. Additionally, EPE plans to auction off an additional 23,742 MW of capacity through 2019. Between 2009 and 2019, the amount of power transmission lines (PTL) will grow from 95,582 km to 132,379 km, a 38 percent increase, representing investments of approximately US$22 billion. The construction of the world's largest high voltage direct current PTL to connect the Madeira River hydro power plants to southeastern states of Brazil will begin in 2011. It will be a 2,383 km-long power line with 5,000 transmission towers, 20,000 km of cables, 433,000 insulators, and many other types of equipment. Public-private partnerships are expected to be the best means of market access for new-to-market U.S. companies interested in future power transmission auctions. Estimates by the Acende Brasil Institute show that Brazilians pay a total of US$68 billion a year for their electrical power. As about 47 percent of this amount is made up of federal, state, and municipal taxes, it is estimated that the power distribution subsector's gross revenues amount to approximately US$32 billion per year. Although there are no official statistics showing planned investments by the power distribution subsector, the "Light for All" rural electrification program launched in 2004 is one of this sub sector's most important programs. Total investment under this program thus far is estimated at US$7.6 billion. By the end of 2010, more than 2.6 million homes have been connected to Brazil's power grid, reaching a total of 13 million Brazilian citizens previously living without electricity in rural areas throughout Brazil. From 2011 to 2014, the program is expected to connect an additional 495,000 Brazilian homes to electric power.

Besides this "Light for All" program, power distributors will continue to invest in power distribution system upgrades and more efficient operational and management systems to make their companies more competitive, and to meet more stringent regulations concerning client satisfaction and client servicing. Companies will also have to continue to invest 0.5 percent of their annual net revenues in energy efficiency and R&D programs.

In the power generation subsector, best sales prospect opportunities include the supply of control and supervision equipment, rectifiers, converters, inverters, heat recovery steam generators and condensers, power generation sets, heat exchangers, gas and steam turbines and parts, and wind power turbines above 1.5 MW. To a lesser extent, solar energy related equipment can also offer longer-term opportunities in Brazil, including liquid pumps for photovoltaic (PV) generation, air cooling systems, photovoltaic panels, solar inverters and batteries, as well as their parts. Additionally, U.S. power generation and transmission operators with a legal presence in Brazil may participate in future power auctions that will be held in 2011 and the following years. The power distribution subsector offers equipment sales potential for lightning arresters, ground and surge protection systems, relays, insulated electric conductors, surge suppressors, and innovative technologies to reduce technical and commercial losses, including smart grid technologies. Over the longer term, industry sources predict that Brazil will need to invest about US$15 billion to implement a smart grid network to increase Brazil's interconnected power grid's efficiency and reliability (e.g. to reduce power black-outs). The first step will be the installation of specific electronic meters, currently under-going the approval process by Brazil's Power Regulator ANEEL. Also, according to ANEEL, there are seven R&D smart grid projects currently underway with a total investment of approximately US$15 million.

Oil and Gas

Brazil's 2010 proven oil reserves reached 12.9 billion barrels and gas reserves totaled to 377 billion cubic meters (m3). Industry sources estimate that beyond the proven figures, Brazil has additional probable oil reserves of 60-80 billion barrels. Such figures take into account the recent discoveries in Brazil's sub-salt layer. In 2010, Brazil produced 2 million barrels of oil per day (bpd) and 62.8 million cubic meters of gas per day. About 92 percent of Brazil's oil production in 2010 originated from offshore fields, mostly at extreme depths. Petrobras's oil and gas production accounts for nearly 95 percent of Brazil's total production. Petrobras owns the majority oil concessions, and will spend US$224 billion (or approximately US$ 44.8 billion/year). Additionally, because it will become the sole operator in future offshore pre-salt tenders, most opportunities for U.S. firms lie in offering services or products to Petrobras. Other oil companies (e.g. Shell, Statoil, Anadarko, Chevron, OGX, etc) will be investing US$ 26 billion in Brazil from 2009 to 2013 (or about US$ 5.2 billion a year). A recent Booz and Company study predicts that total expenditure (investment and operation) in Brazil's oil and gas sector will reach US$400 billion through 2020.

Brazil ranks 16th globally in proven oil reserves and 9th in oil production. It is not a member of the Organization of Petroleum Exporting Countries (OPEC). In 2007, Petrobras discovered significant deepwater oil and gas reserves. These large finds, called the pre-salt fields, are located 200 miles off Brazil's southern coast and lie approximately 7,000 feet below the ocean surface. As these logistically and technologically challenging discoveries are exploited, Brazil will likely become a major oil and gas exporter.

In 2010, Brazil exported 230,492,050 barrels of oil (or, approximately 631,485 bpd). During the same period, Brazil refined about 1.9 million bpd, 338,763 bpd of which were light oil imported to mix with Brazil's predominantly heavy crude. Industry sources estimate that Brazil has probable reserves of 60 to 80 billion barrels and an additional possible 20 to 30 billion barrels. Such figures take into account the recent discoveries in Brazil's sub-salt layer. According to the Brazilian Petroleum Institute, longer-term equipment and service procurement and operational expenses from all oil companies (Petrobras and others) could exceed one trillion dollars through 2020, to develop all of the wells in the Brazilian pre-salt fields. As an example, a field like Tupi, with estimated reserves of eight billion barrels of oil, will require an approximate investment of US$ 50 billion through the lifecycle of that field.

Petrobras' Fleet Modernization and Expansion Program – PROMEF I and II:

Under this program, Petrobras is ordering 26 large vessels to transport oil, by-products and liquefied petroleum gas (LPG), for delivery by 2013. Phase II of the PROMEF calls for purchase of another 23 large vessels, including bunker, LPG and other vessels, for delivery by 2014. Additionally, under the Petrobras 3rd fleet renewal plan, the company will be contracting 146 platform supply and support vessels and boats.

Between 2010 and 2015, Petrobras will spend US$224 billion (or approximately US$ 44.8 billion/year), which represents a 28.4 percent increase over its spending in its previous five-year business plan. About 95 percent (US$ 212.3 billion) of that total spending will be invested in projects in Brazil. The company's oil production is projected to reach 3.9 million bpd by 2014, and 5.4 million bpd by 2020. The E&P segment will command the highest level of spending with approximately US$ 118.8 billion to be invested. The new five-year business plan calls for 16 floating production and offloading platforms and/or modules and 28 offshore drilling rigs which are currently, or, soon to be in the tender process.

Petrobras will also revamp and upgrade a number of existing refineries and will build four new refineries, including a refinery/petrochemical complex that alone calls for a US$8.5 billion investment. Total planned expenditures by 2014 in the entire downstream segment, including gas pipelines and oil, bio-fuels, and gas terminals, will be US$73.6 billion. The petrochemicals subsector will be the third in terms of total planned investment of US$ 17.8 billion.

Moreover, Petrobras plans to increase its production of ethanol and biodiesel by investing US$3.5 billion in that sub-sector through 2014. Other oil companies: The Booz and Company study shows that other oil companies (e.g. Shell, Statoil, Anadarko, Chevron, OGX, etc) will be investing US$ 26 billion in Brazil from 2009 to 2013 (or about US$ 5.2 billion a year). Since state-owned Petrobras' monopoly ended in 1998, 72 firms - half of which are foreign companies - started doing business in Brazil and competed for the 819 oil blocks awarded through ten annual oil-concession licensing rounds. The last auction occurred in December 2008. Petrobras won the majority of these concessions, and because it will become the sole operator in future offshore pre-salt tenders, most opportunities for U.S. firms lie in offering services or products to Petrobras. In 2009, China extended a US$10 billion credit line to Petrobras to develop off-shore oil resources that will be repaid through the export of oil, effectively making China Brazil's first client for its pre- salt oil. In 2009, the U.S. Ex-Im Bank issued a US$2 billion preliminary commitment to Petrobras that will facilitate exporting U.S. oil and gas equipment and services to Brazil.

A new pre-salt regulatory regime was approved by President Lula on December 22, 2010. The new regulatory regime establishes that all future-tendered pre-salt reserves will belong to the Brazilian government and that future pre-salt fields and areas judged strategic for the Brazilian government will be ruled through production sharing agreements (PSAs). The exploration of the fields will be done through consortia, where Petrobras will hold at least 30 percent equity in each oil block. Additionally, Petrobras will be the operator in all future oil fields. In specific cases, as decided by the Brazilian National Energy Council, Petrobras may be called upon to explore selected pre-salt oil fields without a tender process. To date, 29 percent of the pre-salt area has been auctioned off through the previous concession regime. The new PSA legislation will regulate the remaining 71 percent of the pre-salt fields. The consortia will share the produced oil with the Brazilian government and will pay royalties. The division of the oil royalties among the 26 Brazilian States and the Federal District (formed by Brasilia, the capital of Brazil, and surrounding cities) is yet to be determined by the Federal Government.

Safety and Security

Brazil has an extensive and well-developed security market that has consistently registered an average annual growth of 15-20% with annual sales around the US$29 billion. High crime rates and general concern with personal security have increased the demand for security equipment and services. As a result, Brazil's public safety and security market is expected to continue growing in 2011. Brazilian government officials are confident that high-tech security equipment and the deployment of dozens of the thousands of police will ensure security for the 2014 World Cup and subsequently for the Olympics Games 2016. Brazil will invest over $3 billion in domestic security projects in preparation for the World Cup and Olympic Games.

The market for electronic security equipment is estimated at US$1.8 billion. According to a study compiled by the Brazilian Association of Electronic Security Companies the electronic security market has registered average annual growth rates of 20% for several years, and is expected to continue at this pace for some time. The Brazilian electronic security equipment market is highly fragmented, with a large number of both multinational and national players (and a stronger presence of the former). The Closed Circuit TV (CCTV) and access control segments offer high growth potential; however, black market products have made significant inroads in this market, especially in low-end segments. Security is also a concern for the 2014 World Cup and the Brazilian government is studying how best to address it. According to a recent report in a leading newspaper, Folha de Sao Paulo, the government will spend US$1 billion on a range of World Cup-specific investments in the sector, including specialized police equipment and training. The final figure will be determined once the host cities make final decisions about their stadium and urban transportation projects; these projects will vary considerably from city to city.

According to JPMorgan, Brazil is the fifth-largest security market in the world. Foreign products account for approximately 50% of total market share, with U.S. products representing approximately 40% of these imports. This equates to a market worth roughly US$300 million per year. Major foreign competitors include Israel, Korea and Japan, each responsible for about 10- 15% of the import market share.

Best prospects for U.S. companies include access control, closed circuit television systems (CCTVs), alarm systems, surveillance technology, drug and explosive detectors, metal detectors, fire prevention and detection systems, cellular telephone blockers, biometrics, and home security equipment. Financial institutions are the market's main end-users, spending approximately US$1 billion per year on security equipment and services. These institutions are highly sophisticated, demanding quality, warranties and after-sales service. Port and airport security is another high-quality segment; although it has continuously implemented improved security measures, it is expected to continue to offer excellent opportunities for U.S. suppliers. Vehicle surveillance has seen rapid growth over the last few years. According to the press, more than 330,000 cars are stolen in Brazil every year, and carjackings and cargo thefts are also a problem.

Other promising niches are small businesses and private homes as high crime rates force individual citizens and business owners to increase their security expenditures. These end-users, however, usually buy less expensive and less sophisticated equipment. Specialists estimate that Brazil has around five million homes that ought to have some type of security device, but only seven percent are equipped with electronic security systems. Brazilian government officials are focusing attention on providing adequate security for the 2014 World Cup and the Olympics Games 2016. Based on the security investment for the Athens, Sydney, and Beijing Olympic Games, Brazil expects to invest $1.4 billion for security of the World Cup and Olympic venues.

Best prospects in the public segment include radio and communication equipment, consultancy services for image control centers, cameras and control centers with digital recording and monitors, software and hardware, localization systems (GPS), such as digital map software and satellite localization system (for police department vehicles and precincts), investigation software, license plate readers, biometric equipment (facial recognition, fingerprint recognition and iris recognition equipment, despite the high price of such devices), cellular phone call blocking systems for prisons, metal detectors, bullet proof vests (grades II and III), pepper spray, fluorescent vests (for highway patrol and firefighters), fire protection equipment, and shooting range simulators. The Brazilian Government will also invest in developing Command and Control Centers (C4I), establishing a permanent unified public security center for the 2014 World Cup and 2016 Olympic Games, and to serve as a strategic hub for all public security operations. The Brazilian Government has considered building 27 C4Is, one in each state, and a national center (which will act as central command center). The integrated management model will involve the entire police force and security forces, such as firefighters, municipal guards and traffic agents. They will also call on agencies that are not normally considered to be part of public security, such as the National Sanitary Agency (ANVISA) and the Brazilian Airport Infrastructure Company (Infraero).

The public safety & security sector in Brazil is divided into three police forces: civil police, military police and federal police. There is also

Brazil's "Civil Defense" that includes fire departments and the emergency medical rescue department. (Note: "Military Police" is something of a misnomer in that it is not part of Brazil's military, but instead it is a state level police force that uses a rank system similar to that of a military organization). The Ministry of Justice is responsible for public safety & security in Brazil.

There are approximately 8,000 security companies in Brazil divided as follows:
• 48.63% retailers and installers;
• 29.85% provider of monitoring services;
• 12.45% distributors
• 9.07% manufacturers

Roughly 84 percent of Brazil's electronic security is made up of small and micro businesses, though most revenues are generated by a handful of large players. International companies such as Bosch, Johnson Controls, Tyco, Siemens, Pelco, Samsung, GE, Siemens and many others have already established a strong presence in the country through representatives, distributors, and/or joint-venture partners. These companies enjoy good market receptivity among large Brazilian corporations that demand quality, durability, and state-of-the-art technology.

To be successful in Brazil, U.S. manufacturers must either establish themselves within the country or have a well-informed local representative. It is also important to have a distributor or system integrator who can offer after sales and maintenance services, replacement parts, and repairs. Due to the size of the country, most distributors and system integrators in Brazil cover specific regions. They are usually small to medium-sized companies that lack financial capability to invest heavily in product promotion, training, and translation of technical manuals. Therefore, it is important that the U.S. companies provide support for these activities. U.S. companies that have enjoyed the greatest success in Brazil have worked closely with their agents and distributors, investing heavily in market development, product promotion, and personnel training.

In general, goods and equipment used for public security (police and army) are exempt from duties once the Brazilian Army's Procurement Office for Defense and Security Products approves the product specifications. However, some state organizations (e.g. for example, the police in the state of São Paulo) do not import directly from foreign suppliers, but instead purchase from Brazilian-based distributors. In such cases, US exports would accrue import duties when selling to a distributor.

According to local trade contacts, there are no specific technical standards required by the Brazilian government for electronic security equipment. However, U.S. equipment with certifications issued in the United States are more marketable to high-end clients such as financial institutions and some industrial and commercial establishments. Nevertheless, Brazilian legislation requires Portuguese translation of all technical manuals. Although there are no official regulations and technical standards for electronic security equipment, ABESE (a Brazilian trade association for businesses in the field of electronic security systems) created a certification called "Selo Amarelo de Qualidade" (a quality seal). This certification is presently the only quality assurance that consumers have with regards to electronic security companies. The certification is issued by ABESE for companies in the electronic security sector: producers, distributors, and service companies. The certificate takes into consideration the management of the company itself and not the products used or produced by the company.

In order for a company to qualify for the certificate it needs to: (1) be associated with ABESE; (2) be in the electronic security market for over a year; (3) attend ABESE's two-day seminar on professional development; and (4) be audited by the Carlos Alberto Vanzolini Foundation, a renowned certifying organization in Brazil. All imports in Brazil are subject to a number of taxes and fees, which are usually paid during the customs clearance process. In addition, there are other costs and fees such as the warehousing cost, terminal handling fee, customs brokers' union fee, customs brokerage fee, transportation and bank costs, that together usually come to approximately 78 percent of the FOB price. US companies interested in this market segment will find excellent opportunities if they establish themselves in Brazil, or find a joint venture or technology transfer partner in Brazil. The Brazilian legislation for government tenders provides that the lowest bidder wins the contract. Since Brazil has high import-related costs, it is difficult for foreign suppliers to compete successfully in the market unless they consider local production.

Environmental Technologies

Environmental experts estimate that Brazil's environmental technologies market (including equipment, engineering / consulting services, instrumentation, construction and clean up services) is roughly estimated at US$ 10 billion, of which US$ 5.5 billion is related to the water and wastewater subsector; solid waste management at US$ 3.5 billion and air pollution control at US$ 1 billion.

There is currently in Brazil an increasing demand for effluent treatment and energy/water saving technologies, as well as for specialized consulting services. Such technologies include advanced water treatment (filtration), water loss prevention solutions, "intelligent valves", efficient water distribution and reuse projects, water saving devices, and rain water systems, among others. Membrane filtration is a technology that has become more common in Brazil as a consequence of cost reduction. Membranes used in ultra, micro, nano filtration and reverse osmosis are imported into Brazil.

Suppliers of water treatment stations incorporate specific imported equipment; laboratory and analytical equipment are also usually imported, and in an increasing demand. Opportunities include solutions related to water distribution systems, including services and equipment, since the water loss rate in Brazil corresponds to about 40% of the potable water produced in the urban areas. Additionally, water reuse is becoming increasingly important in Brazil, especially in the large centers where water scarcity represents high operational costs for water impounding and adduction. Existing legislation imposing charges for collecting and disposing effluents in water bodies increases the demand for specialized consulting services and effluent treatment technologies.

Investments in solid waste treatment technologies and waste to energy projects in sanitary and hazardous landfills are expanding significantly. The Brazilian Government plans to invest US\$ 870 million in solid waste treatment projects, replacement of garbage dumps, and introduction of selective waste collection services and financing of cooperatives of waste collectors. The Brazilian government expects that recycling activities income increases from current US\$ 1.1 billion to US\$ 4.5 billion. The demand for air pollution control products is also rising in Brazil. In addition to the industrial demand, the increased number of Clean Development Mechanism CDM projects in sanitary landfills and the vehicle emission inspection program, mandatory in some of Brazil's largest municipalities generate a demand for gas emission monitoring technologies and gas analyzers, as well as the demand for industrial filters.

In 2010, the Government of Brazil passed the National Solid Waste Policy (Law 12,305) to stimulate recycling and manage waste with high contamination potential. The law determines that households in municipalities that offer "selective collection services", sort their domestic waste. In order to receive any Government funding for urban cleaning and waste management activities, the municipalities will need to have a waste management plan in place. The law still requires implementation legislation and the companies will need time to adapt to the new requirements and determine the appropriate treatment for each type of material.

Major elements of the National Solid Waste Policy:

1- New garbage dumps cannot be created;

2- All municipalities have to build sanitary landfills that will only allow products that are not appropriate for reuse or composting;

3- Imports of waste are prohibited;

4- Using "reverse logistics" manufacturers, distributors and retailers are obliged to collect certain used products, including agricultural chemicals, batteries, tires, lubricant oils, all types of lamps and electronic products such a cel phone and comptuers;

5- Should manufacturers, importers, distributors and retailers not fulfill their reverse logistics responsibility under the law, the government will fulfill them or contract to have them fulfilled and charge companies accordingly;

6- Recycling industries will have priority in government financing;

7- Encouraged activities are non-generation, reduction, reuse, recycling, treatment and adequate final disposal;

8- Non-recycled waste must be used for energy generation, once technical and environmental feasibility studies indicate the appropriateness. The emission of toxic gases have to be monitored;

9- Companies that manage, transport, store or process hazardous waste must register in the "National Registry of Hazardous Waste Operators" and prove their technical capability.

Water/Waste Water Sector:

The Brazilian government's goal is to provide sanitation coverage to all Brazilian population.

The amount of investments required to reach this objective is US$ 100.5 billion. The sector's major challenge is the expansion of sewage collection and treatment, which is expected to attract most of the investments.

As a result of the Public Consortium Law of 2007 (Law 11455, which creates public- private partnerships as part of the "Sanitation for All" program), the private sector is increasing its direct participation in the sanitation business by operating water and wastewater utilities, which in turn is increasing the demand for higher technology equipment used by the water and wastewater utilities. According to industry specialists, Law 866, which regulates procurement of public sector companies in Brazil, stipulates that procurements favor the lowest bidder. This legislation discourages local water and wastewater product manufacturers and exporters from offering sophisticated technologies.

In 2008, Sabesp, the state of Sao Paulo's water utility, established its first Public-Private-Partnership (PPP) with CAB-Galvao

Consortium. They are now considering Five additional PPPs which are currently being analyzed. In 2007, the municipality of Rio Claro, state of Sao Paulo, established a PPP with the Odebrecht Group, to operate and expand sewage treatment. This was the first municipal PPP in Brazil. Estimates by the Brazilian Association of Water and Sewage Public Services Concessionaires (ABCON) indicate the private sector will invest about US$ 8.3 billion in basic sanitation works by 2017 and will manage concessions that will cover 30% of the Brazilian population, compared to the current level of 9.6%.

The Odebrecht group has recently created its own sanitation company – Odebrecht Engenharia Ambiental (OEA), which already has seven concession contracts in the sector. According to the company's source, OEA has about US$ 690 million to invest in new concessions in the next three years. The Spanish-owned OHL Meio Ambiente Brasil, which currently has two sewage treatment contracts with municipalities in the state of Sao Paulo (Ribeirao Preto and Moji Mirim), foresees investments of US$ 16 million by 2010, for treating half of the sewage of Mogi Mirim (84,000 inhabitants). OHL has investment plans of US$276 million and plans to bid on five new concessions in the mid-term. The municipal water utility in Campinas, Sanasa, will build two sewage treatment plants using Membrane Bioreactor technology (MBR), a technology first promoted in Brazil by USTA which took state water treatment personnel to the U.S. to see the equipment being used.

Mining

Brazil is the world's fifth largest mineral producer and has one of the world's largest mining equipment markets. The mining sector in Brazil expanded quickly from 2000 to mid-2008, breaking records for nearly all categories of mineral exports in almost all years. However, in mid-2008 the international demand for Brazilian minerals, and in 2009 the Brazilian mineral output fell by more than 10% (in volume), especially iron ore. In 2010, a slow but steady recovery took place, and production levels for most minerals are now near or above the record highs of 2008. As a result, local mining companies had a record year in 2010. China has played a very important role for Brazilian mining companies in recent years, and is now the largest importer of Brazil's most important mineral (iron ore). Most of the new mining projects developed in Brazil in recent years were based upon supplying China with iron ore.

Brazil's mineral potential still has not been fully surveyed, and significant discoveries of mineral deposits are still expected in the future. Most of Brazil's mines are open pit so the underground mining equipment market is relatively small. However, more underground mines are expected to open in the next 3-7 years. Brazil's largest installed mining operations are for iron ore, with 2009 output at nearly 350 million metric tons/year (metric t/y), representing nearly 17% of the world's total.

Brazil also produces:
- bauxite (27 million metric tons/year [t/y] in 2009, or 13% of the world's total),
- gold (55 tons per year in 2009 or 2.5% of the world's total),

- kaolin (3 million metric t/y or 6% of the world's total),
- manganese (2.5 million metric t/y or 18% of the world's total),
- niobium (86,000 t/y, with 94% of the world reserves and 96% of the output),
- potassium chloride (KCl) (700,000 t/y),
- phosphate concentrate (6 mil. metric t/y of concentrate),
- zinc (200,000 t/y of metal content or 1.8% of the world's total)
- lead (25,000 tons of primary lead and 142,000 tons of recycled lead),
- copper (220,000 tons of ore),
- tin (15,000 tons of Sn content),
- nickel (85,000 tons Ni content),
- uranium (380 tons of U3O8 concentrate),
- and raw materials for cement (55 million metric t/y of cement in 2010).

Brazil's coal production is relatively small and had been stagnant for the last 20 years. The output in 2009 was only 7 million metric tons of steam coal (compared to 5 million metric tons in 1991), but predicted to reach 12 million metric tons by 2014, in order to supply several new local coal power plants. Total Brazilian deposits of coal are estimated to be 32 billion metric tons. There are 8 coal power plants currently in operation in Brazil, with a combined capacity of 1.4 MW, equivalent to only 1.3% of the country's total electricity consumption. There are projects by local companies to open several new coal power plants in Brazil in the next 5 years, for a combined capacity of 4,000 MW.

Brazil is one of the largest importers of metallurgical coal, used basically by its steel manufacturers. The country imports approximately 16 million metric tons/year (US $2 billion value) of metallurgical coal. The main supplying countries have been Australia, U.S., Canada, and South Africa. The largest Brazilian mining company, Vale, has made large investments in coal mining in Australia and in Mozambique the last four years, and these mines yielded an output of 5.4 million metric tons of coal in 2009. The total deposits in these mines are 2.5 billion metric tons and the total production is predicted to reach 40 million metric tons per year. In 2008, Vale also bought a coal mine in Colombia, which will start producing 4.8 million metric tons per year by late 2011.

Brazil has a very limited market for machinery, as a number of leading multinational manufacturers have factories in country, with many of them even exporting part of their production. For example, Caterpillar has a huge factory in Brazil, with total sales of more than US$2 billion/year, and it exports more than 50% of its Brazilian-made machines all over the world. The same applies to many other world market leaders, such as Cummins, P&H MinePro, Ingersoll Rand, GE, Goodyear, Terex, 3M, Eaton, ITT, Bucyrus Erie, Timken (US), Volvo, Scania Vabis, Tamrock, Sandvik, Asea Brown Bovery, Atlas Copco, SKF (Sweden), Case New Holland, Iveco, FIAT (Italy), Siemens, Liebherr, Schenk Process, Voith, Mercedes Benz, Wehr, Thyssen Krupp, Kuttner, Koch, MAN, Schaeffler (Germany), Michelin Tires, Alstom, Saint Gobain (France), Toshiba, NSK (Japan), Metso, Outokumpu (Finland), Orica (Australia), JCB (UK).

Companies manufacturing in Brazil, however, provide excellent opportunities for U.S. manufacturers of parts and components for mining equipment, such as earth-moving machines, belt conveyors, crushers and grinding equipment, laboratory instruments, drill bits and geological surveying equipment. Best market prospects are for products or components that do not have a similar product made in Brazil. If there is local competition for a product, the imported product will have to offer much higher technology or other benefits relative cost compared to the locally made product, as Brazilian mining companies tend to prefer buying locally even if the products are of lower quality.

Several Brazilian companies have developed their own technologies. The largest ones are Randon, Villares, Bardella, Dedini, Jaraguá, and Isomonte. Hundreds of medium- sized Brazilian companies also specialize in manufacturing all types of parts and components for the suppliers of turn-key equipment. Companies manufacturing in Brazil have the natural advantage of proximity to their end-users.

Foreign manufacturers on the other hand, in addition to language and cultural barriers, have to cope with high import taxes and long import procedures, which often make their products too expensive for the local end-users.

Vale (Companhia Vale do Rio Doce):

Brazil's largest, and the world's second largest, mining company is Companhia Vale do Rio Doce, known as Vale. Privatized in 1997, VALE is responsible for more than 50% of Brazil's mineral output based on value, and represents an excellent opportunity for US equipment suppliers. Vale produces nearly 90% of Brazil's iron ore output; 100% of potash; 85% of manganese; 43% of kaolin; 80% of bauxite; and it is also the top producer of aluminum, copper, and nickel production. Vale is also the leading logistics company for the mining sector in Brazil, especially for ports and railroads, not only for its own use, but also as a supplier of logistics services to other companies. In the last seven years, Vale has diversified globally, having bought the Canadian company INCO (the world's largest nickel producer); plus coal projects in Australia and Mozambique, in addition to exploring many other projects in Latin America, Africa and Asia.

Anglo American has two large iron ore projects in Brazil. The first one is located in Amapá (north of Brazil) and is planning to expand output from one to four million tons in the next 3 years. The second one is in Minas Gerais, planned to start up in 2012 with an output of 26 million tons. Anglo also has a big nickel project named "Barro Alto," started in 2010 with an output of 36,000 kt/year in ferro-nickel alloys.

AngloGold Ashanti is the second largest gold producer in Brazil, with an output of 480,000 troy ounces in 2010, and projects to increase its output in Brazil to 670,000 troy ounces in the next three years.

MMX is a new company that had started three large iron ore projects in Brazil in 2007, and has sold most of them to Anglo American. It currently has an output of nearly 9 million t/y of iron ore, and has a new "Bom Sucesso" project for 9 million t/y for start-up in 2014.

Usiminas, Brazil's largest steel manufacturer, has a current output of currently 7 million metric tons of iron ore, and has a project to expand to 29 mil. metric tons by 2015, in a joint-venture with the Japanese company Sumitomo.

CSN is the second largest Brazilian steel producer, producing 25 milmion metric tons per year of iron ore, with a project to expand its output to 40 mil. metric t/y. ArcelorMittal is Brazil's third largest steel producer. The company had an output of 4 mil. metric tons of iron ore in 2009, being expanded to 10 mil. metric tons in 2012. Samarco: is co-owned by CVRD (50%) and BHP (50%). The company produces 17 million metric tons per year of iron ore pellets.

Gold: The total Brazilian output of gold is expected to expand from 54 t/y in 2008 to 100 t/y of gold in 2013, according to the Brazilian Ministry of Energy and Mines. The Canadian Kinross Group became Brazil's largest gold producer in 2008, when it started up a new project of US$ 550 million and increased its output of gold metal from 5.4 to 17.2 metric tons / year. The largest producers of gold in Brazil in 2009 were Kinross with 429,000 troy ounces, AngloGold Ashanti with 406,000 troy ounces, Yamana Gold with 333,000 troy ounces, Jaguar Mining with 155,000 troy ounces and Vale with 49,000 troy ounces.

Votorantim: This Brazilian group is the only local producer of zinc, with a 40% share, and of is also a big producer of bauxite and aluminum.

MRN is the largest producer of bauxite in the world, with production of 18 million metric tons per year. It is owned by Vale (40%), BHP Billiton Metals (14,8%), Alcan (12%), CBA (10%), Alcoa (13.58%), Norsk Hydro (5%), and Abalco (4.62%).

In order to have good relations with the local mining companies, it is absolutely necessary for foreign equipment manufacturers to have some degree of a local presence in Brazil. Most multinational manufacturers of mining equipment have factories in Brazil, as explained above. Smaller companies that cannot afford to establish a local subsidiary must at least have a good Brazilian representative that can supply or subcontract technical maintenance and some degree of local assembling. The mining companies, even the very large ones, prefer to contact the Brazilian representative and do all the import procedures through them, instead of contacting the foreign suppliers directly. This is especially due to the language barrier and to bureaucratic import procedures.

Price and just-in-time delivery for components are the key factors for most importers. Some large mining companies have their own bonded warehouses, and their products will go through customs and pay import duties only when the products are needed. Labor is relatively cheap in Brazil, compared to the U.S., so expensive equipment that makes redundant large numbers of employees is not necessarily financially attractive to Brazilian companies. U.S. companies looking for a good occasion to meet Brazilian mining companies should consider the Brazilian mining show Exposibram, as listed below. Mining officials from all over Brazil travel specifically to attend this event. Import duties in Brazil are high in comparison with other countries. The import duty on mining equipment is normally between 5 to 12%, calculated based on the CIF (cost, insurance and freight) price.

Medical Equipment

Brazil is the largest medical equipment market in South America. The total market for medical equipment in Brazil should continue to expand approximately 10% through 2011. Brazil is both a major medical equipment producer and importer. This industry is comprised of a number of related products and services, including:

Medical equipment and devices.

Dental equipment and products.

Radiological and diagnostic imaging equipment.

Laboratory equipment.

Brazilian medical equipment revenues in 2010 reached an estimated US$ 5.0 billion. The United States accounts for approximately 30% of the import market, with U.S. sales mainly going through local agents, distributors and importers who sell to hospitals and clinics. The market for electro medicine equipment is around US$200 million, which represents approximately 50% of total sales in Latin America. In 2010, imports for In Vitro Diagnostics reagents and devices increased approximately 55% as demand recovered from 2008 economic downturn.

There are few high-quality Brazilian manufacturers of advanced medical products, so Brazil's reliance on imports should continue for some time. Local buyers view US and other foreign products (mainly Canadian and European) as having comparable quality and reliability. Thus, financing terms often become the differentiating criteria in making a sale.

Brazil's strengthened currency has meant that private and public hospitals have greater purchasing power, and with continued expansion of Brazil's private health care sector, the market should grow. Approximately 80% of all products used in hospitals have no similar manufacturing in the country and must be imported. New opportunities for US exporters abound, particularly for advanced medical equipment, disposables, diagnostic devices, implants and components.

The market for home health care products has been increasing in recent years. Brazilian health insurance companies are responsible for paying 99% of the costs related to home care treatment, and as such, the U.S. Commercial Service sees the market for home health care products growing dramatically during the coming years. Brazil's Regional Nursing Council is currently developing procedures on how to regulate this market, including standards for health professionals.

In addition to the attractive size of the Brazilian medical market, US exporters should consider the opportunities offered by Mercosur, and use Brazil as a "spring board" for export into Argentina, Uruguay and Paraguay.

Architecture/Engineering/Construction
The 2014 soccer World Cup, the 2016 summer Olympics, and other international games to be hosted by Brazil over the next few years, will

generate numerous business opportunities in the 12 cities hosting games, particularly in the Architecture/Engineering/Construction (ACE) sector.

The Government of the State of Rio de Janeiro estimates that investments in the State from 2011 to 2016 will reach at least US$ 50 billion, in sectors including building and sports infrastructure, transportation, public security, education, catering, leasing, insurance, etc. Many of the projects and investments carried out before the Olympics will be done under Public-Private Partnerships (PPPs).

Investments Planned:
a) For the 2014 World Cup (To be held in 12 Brazilian Cities):
Stadiums: US$ 2.7 billion
Airport renewals: US$ 3 billion (Not including the High Speed Train Rio/Sao Paulo, which might not be ready by 2014, and which is valued at US$ 20 billion)

b) Investments in Sport Facilities (Including World Cup and Olympic Games)

Although more than half of Rio 2016 venues are already in place because Rio hosted the 2007 Pan American Olympic Games, about 20 new facilities will need to be built. These include:

Aquatic sports stadium - US$40 million;

Olympic Park to host gymnastics, cycling, handball, etc. - US$200 million;

Olympic village - US$450 million;

Olympic Tennis Center - US$45 million;

Rowing stadium at Rodrigo de Freitas Lagoon - US$2 million;

Copacabana Beach Volley Arena - US$7 million; and

Maracanã Stadium renovation (for both the World Cup and the Olympic Games):

US$400 million before 2014. The stadium will be used for soccer games and for the opening and closing ceremonies of the 2014 World Cup and the 2016 Rio Olympic Games.

c) Investments in Hotel/Hospital Facilities

Over 30 hotels will be built or renovated to handle the increase in visitors resulting from the Games. Of these 30 hotels, 17 are already licensed and several hotels are already being refurbished. State and Federal tax incentives are being offered to make opportunities for refurbishment, building, acquiring or operating hotels more attractive to investors. In the health care sector, there are plans to build an Olympic Village Clinic and 3 new state-of-the-art hospitals in the city of Rio before the 2016 Olympic Games.

d) Investments in Infrastructure

As above mentioned, the estimated investment in infrastructure for the World Cup and the Olympic Games is slated at US$50 billion, of which US$5 billion will be used for logistics upgrades at seaports and airports.

The main infrastructure projects include:

Modernizing and enlarging two airport terminals;

Highway widening to accommodate "Olympic lanes";

The Port of Rio revitalization of 30,000 square meter leisure area featuring bars, restaurants, an amphitheater, museum, aquarium, a multi-use space and parking;

Port dredging;

Two new subway lines;

Bus Rapid Transit (BRT) system;

Housing projects (to include low income housing); and

Various water sanitation projects.

e) Olympic Committee investments

The Brazilian Olympic Committee will have a budget of approximately US$ 2.5 billion. This budget will be used for the overall organization and management of the Olympic Games and will include such things as supplying the athletes' and 80,000 volunteers with food and transportation, leasing/purchase of a wide range of the sporting equipment needed for the various events, construction of temporary sporting venues, design and construction of permanent state-of-the –art training facilities, permanent athlete and media housing, security/access control and crowd management systems. These projects and activities are still in the planning phase and must be reviewed and approved by the International Olympic Committee. Tenders for these projects and activities will only be opened after 2012 London Olympic Games.

Best prospects for US companies include the following areas:

- Architecture/Engineering/Construction (ACE): Stadiums, hotels, airports, ports, housing, museums: new design and build and renovation of existing facilities;

- Advanced technology: Areas such as ICT, ITS and energy efficiency and green technologies;

- Services: Financial (Banking services, Insurance, Private Equity and Venture Capital, Leasing, Legal, among others.);

- Sport venues and training facilities and sports equipment and services;

Specific tenders directly related to the Military Games have already been issued as have a substantial number of tenders related to the World Cup. However, procurement directly related to the Olympic Games has not yet begun. The Brazilian Olympic Public Authority will be in charge of the overall procurement tied to the Olympic Games and that authority has not yet been assembled by the new Administration but it is expected to be formed over the next few months. There will also be procurement for the

Olympic Games by the Rio City and State Governments and the Brazilian arm of the International Olympic Committee.

The Brazilian Constitution provides that all governmental purchases, at Federal, State and Municipal levels should be contracted through public tenders. This process is regulated by the Brazilian Bid Law (Law # 8,666, introduced in 1993). This law requires any and all official bidders have a legal presence in Brazil. Since practically all procurement related either directly or indirectly to the Olympic Games will be made by Brazilian Governmental entities under Law 8,666, CS Brazil recommends working with us to find a qualified local representative/distributor or Brazilian JV partner now in order to participate in the many business opportunities offered by the Games. Note that among the priorities considered to select a supplier under procurement in Brazil (in the public or private sectors), there are: corporate and social responsibility; ethical practices (client privacy, information management issues) and environmental aspects.

Chapter 4: Trade Regulations and Standards

Import Tariffs

Imports are subject to a number of taxes and fees in Brazil, which are usually paid during the customs clearance process. There are three taxes that account for the bulk of import costs: the Import Duty (II), the Industrialized Product tax (IPI) and the Merchandise and Service Circulation tax (ICMS). In addition to these taxes, several smaller taxes and fees apply to imports. Note that most taxes are calculated on a cumulative basis.

Brazil and its Southern Common Market (Mercosur) partners, Argentina, Paraguay and Uruguay, implemented the Mercosur Common External Tariff (CET) on January 1, 1995. Each country maintains a separate exceptions list of items for tariffs. In 1995 Brazil implemented the Mercosur Common Nomenclature, known as the NCM (Nomenclatura Comum do Mercosur), consistent with the Harmonized System (HS) for tariff classification.

The Brazilian Government established a computerized information system to monitor imports and to facilitate customs clearance known as the Foreign Trade Integrated System (SISCOMEX). SISCOMEX has facilitated and reduced the amount of paperwork previously required for importing into Brazil. Brazilian importers must be registered in the Foreign Trade Secretariat's (SECEX's) Export and Import Registry and receive a password given by Customs to operate the SISCOMEX. The SISCOMEX creates electronic import documents and transmits information to a central computer.

Import Duty (II)
The Import duty is a federally mandated product specific tax levied on a CIF (Cost, Insurance, and Freight) basis. In most cases, Brazilian import duty rates range from 10% to 35%.
Industrialized Product Tax (IPI)
The IPI is a federal tax levied on most domestic and imported manufactured products. It is assessed at the point of sale by the manufacturer or processor in the case of domestically produced goods, and at the point of customs

clearance in the case of imports. The IPI tax is not considered a cost for the importer, since the value is credited back to the importer. Specifically, when the product is sold to the end user, the importer debits the IPI cost.

The Government of Brazil levies the IPI rate by determining how essential the product may be for the Brazilian end-user. Generally, the IPI tax rate ranges from 0 to 15%. In the case of imports, the tax is charged on the product's CIF value plus import duty. A product's IPI rate is directly proportional to its import tariff rate. As with value-added taxes in Europe, IPI taxes on products that pass through several stages of processing are reduced to compensate for IPI taxes paid at each stage. Brazilian exports are exempt from the IPI tax.

Merchandise and Service Circulation Tax (ICMS)

The ICMS is a state government value-added tax applicable to both imports and domestic products. The ICMS tax on imports is assessed ad valorem on the CIF value, plus import duty, plus IPI. Although importers have to pay the

ICMS to clear the imported product through Customs, it is not necessarily a cost item for the importer because the paid value represents a credit to the importer. When the product is sold to the end user, the importer debits the ICMS, which is included in the final price of the product and is paid by the end user.

Effectively, the tax is paid only on the value-added; the tax is generally passed on to the buyer since it is included in price charged for the merchandise. The ICMS tax due to the state government is based upon taxes collected on sales by a company, minus the taxes paid in purchasing raw materials and intermediate goods. The ICMS tax is levied on both intrastate and interstate transactions and is assessed on every transfer or movement of merchandise. The rate varies among states: in the State of São Paulo, the rate varies from 7 to 18 percent. On interstate movements, the tax will be assessed at the rate applicable to the destination state. Some sectors of the economy, such as mining, electricity, liquid fuels and natural gas can be exempt from the ICMS tax. Most Brazilian exports are exempt.

U.S. exporters and Brazilian importers must register with the Foreign Trade Secretariat (SECEX), an organ of the Ministry of Industrial Development and Commerce (MDIC). Depending on the product, Brazilian authorities may require more documentation. The Ministry of Health controls all products that may affect the human body, including pharmaceuticals, vitamins, cosmetics and medical equipment/devices. Such products can only be imported and sold in Brazil if the foreign company establishes a local Brazilian manufacturing unit or local office, or the foreign company appoints a Brazilian distributor who is authorized by the Brazilian authorities to import and distribute medical products. Such products must be registered with the Brazilian Ministry of Health. The registration process can sometimes be complex and/or time consuming.

At this time, the U.S. Government maintains no export controls specific to Brazil. Normal controls are maintained on military equipment, high-tech information systems, and equipment of a highly sensitive nature. Items on the

Munitions Control List are also a controlled export to nearly all countries worldwide, including Brazil, requiring special licenses from the State Department or Commerce Department depending upon the item.

Since 2000, the Government of Brazil has made an allowance for temporary importation of products that are used for a predetermined time period and then re-exported. The U.S. Commercial Service has seen a number of delays in regards to temporary imports, and continues to work through the "U.S. – Brazil Commercial Dialogue" to counter these problems. The Brazilian Government is studying the adoption of the ATA Carnet, an international customs document that allows importers to temporarily import goods up to one year without payment of normally applicable duties and taxes, including value-added taxes. The adoption of ATA Carnet use in Brazil would have a huge impact on customs clearance for U.S. trade show exhibitors that currently face extreme difficulties and delays in getting these temporary imports into Brazil, often writing off the imports as a complete loss. The ATA Carnet legislation has been submitted to the Brazilian Congress for approval.

Under Brazil's temporary import program, the II and IPI are used to determine the temporary import tax. Products must be used in the manufacture of other goods and involve payment of rental or lease fee from the local importer to the international exporter. There are very strict rules regarding the entry of used merchandise into Brazil. An example of products falling under this program would be the temporary importation of machine tools. The example below shows that taxes due is proportional to the time frame the imported product will remain in Brazil. This also applies to temporary entry of personal belongings.

The Brazilian Customer Protection Code requires that product labeling provide the consumer with precise and easily readable information about the product's quality, quantity, composition, price, guarantee, shelf life, origin, and risks to the consumer's health and safety. Imported products should bear a Portuguese translation of this information.

Products should be labeled in metric units or show a metric equivalent.

The Brazilian Government has eliminated most import prohibitions with certain exceptions. In general, all used consumer goods are prohibited from being imported. Used capital goods are allowed only when there is no similar item produced locally. Aviation parts, for example, are one of the few used products allowed to enter Brazil. Remanufactured goods are still considered used goods, although CS Brazil is working through the "U.S.-Brazil Commercial Dialogue" to address this issue. The country prohibits the imports of beef derived from cattle administered with growth hormones, fresh poultry meat and poultry products coming from U.S. and color prints for the theatrical and television market. There is also specific legislation that prohibits the importation of products that the Brazilian regulatory agencies consider harmful to health, sanity, national security interest, and the environment

It is essential to have all documents in complete order. Products can get caught up for various reasons, including minor errors or omissions in paperwork. Products held at customs in Brazil can be assessed high fees. Brazilian Customs frequently seizes shipments that appear to have inaccurate documentation. Customs has the right to apply fines and penalties at their discretion.

Standards

Brazil has strict rules regarding standards and an active group of standards organizations. The National Institute of Metrology, Standardization and Industrial Quality (INMETRO) is a government entity and is the operating arm of Brazil's standards regime, led by the National Council of Metrology, Standardization and Industrial Quality, CONMETRO. The council is formed by a group of 8 ministries and 5 governmental agencies. The council is the regulatory body of The National System of Metrology, Standardization and Industrial Quality (SINMETRO).

INMETRO is the main national accreditation body and is in charge of implementing the national policies regarding quality and metrology established by the CONMETRO, the council that oversees INMETRO's activities. INMETRO is responsible for certification products, services, licensing and testing labs among other duties. More information about INMETRO can be found at http://www.inmetro.gov.br/english. The Brazilian Association of Technical Standards (ABNT) is also a recognized standards organization. NIST Notify U.S. Service Member countries of the World Trade Organization (WTO) are required under the Agreement on Technical Barriers to Trade (TBT Agreement) to report to the WTO all proposed technical regulations that could affect trade with other member countries. Notify U.S. is a free, web-based e-mail subscription service that offers an opportunity to review and comment on proposed foreign technical regulations that can affect your access to international markets.

Conformity assessment includes all activities needed to demonstrate compliance with specified requirements relating to a technical regulation or voluntary standard. In Brazil, the conformity assessment system follows ISO guidelines. Conformity assessment includes test and calibration laboratories, product certification bodies, accreditation bodies, inspection and verification units, quality system registrars, and others. Conformity assessment can be voluntary or mandatory (done through a legal instrument to protect the consumer on issues related to life, health and environment). Interested U.S. parties can be accredited by INMETRO to perform conformity assessment activities.

Mandatory Testing and Mandatory Product Certification

For regulated products, the relevant government agency generally requires that entities engaged in product testing and mandatory certification be accredited by INMETRO. Generally, testing must be performed in-country, unless the necessary capability does not exist in Brazil.

INMETRO is a signatory to the mutual recognition arrangement (MRA) of the International Laboratory Accreditation Cooperation (ILAC), which can facilitate acceptance of test results from U.S. laboratories that are accredited by U.S. organizations who are also signatories. There is no legal mandate as of yet to retest non-regulated products that have been approved in their country of origin. For non-regulated products, some U.S. marks and product certification may be accepted. As with all voluntary standards, any certification that may be required in non-regulated sectors is a contractual matter to be decided between buyer and seller. Market forces and preferences often lead to the need for a specific certification.

To facilitate U.S. product acceptance in Brazil by recognizing existing certifications, agreements between U.S. and local certifiers/testing houses are encouraged. Also, there is no impediment for the establishment of U.S. certification organizations in Brazil. If your product has been certified in the U.S. or Europe, it probably will not need to be re-certified (see MRA above). The General Coordination for Accreditation (CGCRE) of INMETRO is responsible for accrediting certification bodies, quality system registrars, inspection bodies, product verification and training bodies, as well as testing and calibration laboratories.

The Brazilian Consumer Protection code, in effect since September 12, 1990, requires that product labels provide consumers with correct, clear, precise, and easily readable information about the product's quality, quantity, composition, price, guarantee, shelf life, origin, and risks to the consumer's health and safety. Imported products should bear a Portuguese translation, and all products should use the official metric units or show a metric equivalent.

Trade Agreements

Brazil is a member of the Mercosur trading bloc, which has its own regional standards organization that issues and harmonizes standards. Technical committees write and recommend standards in selected areas. Each country must ratify the standard before they are adopted in that country. A number of standards have already been adopted as Mercosur standards.

Brazil is open to and encourages foreign investment. After a decline in 2009 as a result of the global financial crisis, 2010 foreign direct investment (FDI) into Brazil was predicted to grow to approximately USD 33 billion (see final page for a historical chart of FDI inflows). Brazil is consistently the largest FDI recipient in Latin America and typically receives close to half of all South America's incoming FDI. The United States is a major foreign investor in Brazil. FDI is prevalent across Brazil's economy, although certain sectors -- notably media and communications, aviation, transportation and mining -- are subject to foreign ownership limitations. While Brazil is generally considered a friendly environment for foreign investment, burdensome tax and regulatory requirements exist. In most cases, these impediments apply without discrimination to both foreign and domestic firms. The Government of Brazil (GOB) generally makes no distinction between foreign and national capital.

Supported by strong domestic demand, global demand for commodity exports, a growing middle class, and prudent macroeconomic policies in recent years, Brazil weathered the global financial crisis better than most major economies. While GDP declined by 0.2 percent in 2009, the Brazilian economy was well into recovery in the latter half of the year. Growth continued to rebound in 2010, and full year growth was expected to surpass 7.5 percent. Analysts' predictions anticipate that growth in 2011 will settle around 4.5 percent. In 2010, the Brazilian people elected a new president, Dilma Rousseff, to succeed Luiz Inacio Lula da Silva ("Lula"). Rousseff, who assumed the presidency on January 1, 2011, is of the same political party (PT) as Lula and is generally continuing to follow the economic policies of the previous government Banking: Brazil's banking sector includes significant foreign investment and representation. While the Constitution of 1988 technically forbids new or expanded foreign investment in the banking sector, the vast majority of requests for entry or expansion have been approved on a case-by-case basis. Recent Brazilian Central Bank figures report that in September 2010 foreign banks comprised 19 of the top 50 Brazilian banks in terms of total assets, representing 18.3 percent of total financial assets less brokerage.

Insurance: Since 1996 the insurance sector has been open to foreign investors with most major U.S. firms represented via joint venture arrangements. In 2007, Complementary Law 126 was published in Brazil eliminating the previous state monopoly on reinsurance through the government-owned Brazil Reinsurance Institute (IRB), which had been in place since 1939.

Privatization: Foreign investment has played a significant role in Brazil's privatization programs. From the early 1990s through 2009, Brazil's completed USD 87.8 billion worth of privatizations, and another USD 18.1 billion in related debt transfer off the government accounts. Foreign investment accounted for about USD 42.1 billion of the privatizations. Of this foreign investment, U.S. investors accounted for one third or USD 14.0 billion. After a slowdown in privatization activity in the early 2000s, the Lula administration, which took office in 2003, revived the program with three important transactions: the 2004 privatization of the State Bank of Maranhao for USD 26.6 million, the 2005 privatization of the

State Bank of Ceara for USD 297.9 million, and the 2006 privatization of Paulista Electric Energy Transmission Company for USD 230 million. In 2007 and 2008, large scale infrastructure projects were auctioned, including federal highways, high speed rail, and airports. Additional auctions of infrastructure concessions are expected for 2011-2015.

Ownership Restrictions: A 1995 constitutional amendment terminated the distinction between foreign and local capital in general, but there are laws that restrict foreign ownership within some sectors, notably media and communications and aviation. Foreign investment restrictions remain in a limited number of other sectors, including highway freight (20 percent) and mining of radioactive ore. Foreign ownership of land within 150 km of national borders remains prohibited unless approved by Brazil's National Security Council. In October 2009, the Brazilian Chamber of Deputies approved legislation that would further restrict foreign ownership of land along Brazil's borders and within the Amazon. The proposed legislation still requires passage by the Brazilian Senate, followed by presidential approval before it can become law. On August 23, 2010, the GOB issued a revised interpretation of Brazil's 1971 land ownership legislation (Law 5709) strengthening existing language limiting foreign ownership of agricultural lands in rural municipalities. Depending on how local municipalities enforce them, the new regulations have the potential to disrupt purchases of farmlands by foreigners.

Media: Open broadcast (non-cable) television companies are subject to a regulation requiring that 80 percent of their programming content be domestic in origin. Additionally, Law 10610 (2002) limits foreign ownership in other media, including open broadcast and print media outlets, to 30 percent. Proposed legislation introduced into the Congress in 2007 would liberalize foreign ownership in other electronic communication formats, provided the foreign entity still maintain local operations, but it has not been passed. Foreign ownership of cable companies is limited to 49 percent, and the foreign owner must have a headquarters in Brazil and have had a presence in the country for the previous ten years. National cable and satellite operators are subject to a fixed title levy on foreign content and foreign advertising on their channels. Current legislation, PLC 116, under consideration contains measures that could impose local content requirements for cable operators and pay TV programming.

Aviation: The Government of Brazil currently restricts foreign investment in domestic airline companies to a maximum of 20 percent. In May of 2009, Brazil's Civil Aviation Regulatory Agency (ANAC) proposed increasing foreign ownership in Brazilian airlines to 49 percent, and facilitating quicker entry of new airlines into the Brazilian market. These proposals have not yet been approved by the Brazilian Congress. The Government of Brazil is considering potential privatization of commercial airport operations. The United States and Brazil liberalized cargo and passenger services in June 2008. In March 2011, officials from the U.S. and Brazil signed a new air transport agreement that will remove in 2015, if approved by Brazil's Congress before then, limits on the number of passenger and cargo flights between the two countries. Officials also signed in March 2011 a

Memorandum of Consultations, which took effect upon signature, that established a schedule for increasing between 2011 and 2015 the number of flights allowed between the two countries.

Investment Goals: In May 2008, Brazil published the Productive Development Policy which encourages technological innovations and new investment opportunities in the country. It sets targets for investment spending to reach 21 percent of GDP and private investment in R&D to reach 0.64 percent of GDP by 2010. While investment as a percent of GDP has increased in recent years, Brazil did not reach its targets set in 2008: investment and R&D as a percent of GDP reached an estimated 19 and 0.58 percent respectively in 2010. High level government officials more recently declared a 23 percent of GDP target by 2014, with leading support from the private sector.

There are few restrictions on converting or transferring funds associated with a foreign investment in Brazil. Foreign investors may freely convert Brazilian currency in the unified foreign exchange market wherein buy-sell rates are determined by market forces. All foreign exchange transactions, including identifying data, must be reported to the Central Bank. Foreign exchange transactions on the current account have been fully liberalized.

Foreigners investing in Brazil must register their investment with the Central Bank within 30 days of the inflow of resources to Brazil. Registration is done electronically. Investments involving royalties and technology transfer must be registered with Brazil's patent office, the National Institute of Industrial Property (INPI). Investors must also have a local representative in Brazil. Portfolio investors must have a Brazilian financial administrator and register with the Brazilian Securities Exchange Commission (CVM). All incoming foreign loans must be approved by the Central Bank. In most instances, the loans are automatically approved. Automatic approval is not issued when the costs of the loan are "not compatible with normal market conditions and practices." In such instances, the Central Bank may request additional information regarding the transaction.

Foreign loans obtained abroad do not require advance approval by the Central Bank, provided the recipient is not a government entity. Loans to government entities, however, require prior approval from the Brazilian Senate as well as from the Finance Ministry Treasury Secretariat, and must be registered with the Central Bank. Interest and amortization payments specified in a loan contract can be made without additional approval from the Central Bank. Early payments can also be made without additional approvals, if the contract includes a provision for them. Otherwise, early payment requires notification to the Central Bank to ensure accurate records of Brazil's stock of debt.

Foreign investors, upon registering their investment with the Central Bank, are able to remit dividends, capital (including capital gains), and, if applicable, royalties. Remittances must also be registered with the Central Bank. Dividends cannot exceed corporate profits. The remittance transaction may be carried out at any bank by documenting the source of the transaction (evidence of profit or sale of assets) and showing that applicable taxes have been paid.

Capital gain remittances are subject to a 15 percent income withholding tax, with the exception of the capital gains and interest payments on tax exempt domestically issued Brazilian bonds. Repatriation of the initial investment is also exempt from income tax. Lease payments are assessed a 15 percent withholding tax. Remittances related to technology transfers are not subject to the tax on credit, foreign exchange, and insurance, although they are subject to a 15 percent withholding tax and an extra 10 percent Contribution of Intervention in the Economic Domain (CIDE). Loans with terms of 90 days or less must pay an IOF, a tax on financial operations, of 5.38 percent, while those of longer maturity, profits and FDI remittances must pay an IOF of 0.38 percent. Foreign cable and satellite television programmers are subject to an 11 percent remittance tax; however, the tax can be avoided if the programmer invests 3 percent of its remittances in co-production of Brazilian audio-visual services.

In October of 2009 the GOB imposed a two percent IOF tax on capital inflows by foreigners for portfolio investments, and in November of 2009 the government instituted a 1.5 percent tax when foreign investors convert American Depositary Receipts (ADRs) for Brazilian companies into receipts for shares issued locally in Brazil. In October of 2010 the GOB imposed two consecutive increases to the IOF tax on capital inflows from abroad for fixed income investments; from two percent to four percent, and then from four percent to six percent. The IOF does not apply to direct investment inflows. In October of 2010 the GOB also raised the tax foreigners must pay on margin deposits for futures market trades from 0.38 percent to six percent. The taxes on financial flows were imposed primarily to try and curb increases in the value of the Brazilian currency, and increases in the IOF or additional measures to restrict inflows are possible.

Brazil's strong macroeconomic fundamentals and high real interest rates have driven nearly a 40 percent appreciation of Brazil's currency (the real) against the dollar over the last two years. In addition to the taxes described in the paragraph immediately above, authorities have sought additional measures to control appreciation of the real, including through Central Bank accumulation of over 90 billion dollars in foreign exchange reserves over the last two years.

There have been no expropriation actions in Brazil against foreign interests in the recent past, nor have there been any signs that the current government is contemplating such actions. In the past, some claims regarding land expropriations by state agencies have been judged by courts in U.S. citizens' favor. However, compensation has not always been paid as states have filed appeals to these decisions, and the Brazilian judicial system moves slowly.

The Brazilian court system, in general, is overburdened, and contract disputes can often take years to move through the system. The 2011 World Bank "Doing Business" survey found that on average it takes 45 procedures and

616 days to litigate a contract breach at an average cost of 16.5 percent of the claim. Judicial reform measures enacted in December 2004, however, have streamlined some administrative procedures, and the introduction of the concept of binding precedent should, over time, make judicial decisions more predictable.

Article 34 of Brazilian Law 9.307, the 1996 Brazilian Arbitration Act, defines a foreign arbitration judgment as any judgment rendered outside the national territory. The law established that the Brazilian Federal Supreme Court must ratify foreign arbitration awards. Law 9.307 also stipulates that the foreign arbitration award is to be recognized or executed in Brazil in conformity with the international agreements ratified by the country and, in their absence, with domestic law. (Note: A 2001 Federal Supreme Court ruling established that the 1996 Brazilian Arbitration Act, permitting international arbitration subject to Federal Supreme Court ratification of arbitration decisions, does not violate the Federal Constitution's provision that "the law shall not exclude any injury or threat to a right

from the consideration of the Judicial Power.")
Brazil has ratified the 1975 Inter-American
Convention on International Commercial
Arbitration (Panama Convention), the 1979
Inter-American Convention on Extraterritorial
Validity of Foreign Judgments and Arbitration
Awards (Montevideo Convention) and the 1958
U.N. Convention on the Recognition and
Enforcement of Foreign Arbitration Awards
(New York Convention). Brazil, however, is not
a member of the International Center for the
Settlement of Investment Disputes (ICSID), also
known as the Washington Convention.

Brazil has a commercial code that governs most
aspects of commercial association, except for
corporations formed for the provision of
professional services, which are governed by
the civil code. In 2005, bankruptcy legislation
(Law 11101) went into effect creating a system,
modeled on Chapter 11 of the U.S. bankruptcy
code, which allows a company in financial
trouble to negotiate a restructuring with its
creditors outside of the courts. In the event a
company does fail despite restructuring efforts,
the reforms give creditors improved ability to

recover their debts. Brazil has both a federal and a state court system and jurisprudence is based on civil law. Federal judges hear most disputes in which one of the parties is the State and rule on lawsuits between a foreign State or international organization and a municipality or a person residing in Brazil. Five regional federal courts hear appeals of federal judges' decisions.

The Brazilian government uses a variety of tax incentives and attractive financing through the National Bank for Economic and Social Development (BNDES) to actively encourage both national and foreign investment. With 2010 lending surpassing USD 95 billion, BNDES is the largest development bank in the world. The Bank actively promotes development in traditionally underserved regions of the country and other potentially marginally profitable ventures, but the majority of lending takes place in the more developed regions of the country. In 2010, the Southeast has benefited the most from BNDES financing having received 58 percent of funds distributed, followed by the South with 18 percent, the Northeast 10, the Mid-West 7, and the North 7. The vast majority of the funding (82 percent) has gone to large companies. A 2004 Public-Private Partnership (PPP) investment law promotes joint ventures in otherwise marginally profitable infrastructure investments.

In 2010, the Brazilian government announced a major expansion to the 2007 Program to Accelerate Growth (PAC), the government's national initiative to develop major infrastructure projects. While the implementation and efficiency of the PAC and follow- on PAC-2 have been subject to national debate, major projects have been completed and are in process throughout the country. The government that took office in January 2011 intends to cut 2011 spending from planned levels; such cuts may delay implementation of some PAC and PAC-2 projects. The government continues to indicate it is interested in attracting foreign investment to fund infrastructure projects, including via the March 2010 announced USD 900 billion PAC-2 program, designed to drive infrastructure projects through 2014 and beyond.

The Government of Brazil extends tax benefits for investment in less developed parts of the country, for example the Northeast and the Amazon regions, with equal application to foreign and domestic investors. These incentives have been successful in attracting major foreign plants to areas like the Manaus Free Trade Zone, but most foreign investment remains concentrated in the more industrialized southern part of Brazil. Individual states have sought to attract investment by offering ad hoc tax benefits and infrastructure support to specific companies, negotiated on a case by case basis. These have proven controversial, with other states challenging them as harmful fiscal competition. Tax reform legislation that would limit states' ability to offer special tax incentives to attract investment away from other states has been awaiting congressional action since August 2009.

In 2007, Brazil restored tax breaks to exporters with the enactment of Law 11529 with the stated intention to help industries hurt by the strengthening Real. This law allows certain Brazilian industrial sectors (textiles, furniture, ornamental stones, woodworking, leatherworking, shoes, leather goods, heavy and agricultural machinery manufacturers, apparel and automotive - including automotive parts) to apply PIS-COFINS (social integration program) tax credits for the purchase of capital goods, both domestic and imported, that are used for manufacturing finished products. The law also expands the government's program to exporting companies purchasing capital goods. To be exempt from paying the 9.25 percent PIS-COFINS tax on these purchases, companies normally must prove they derive at least 70 percent of their revenues from exports. This benchmark was lowered to 60 percent for companies in the sectors covered by the legislation.

In May of 2010, the government placed state-owned communications firm Telebras at the head of a National Broadband Plan which incorporates fiscal incentives, private sector participation, and regulatory reform to build-out Brazil's next generation communication infrastructure network. While the plan provides commercial opportunities for the private sector, including foreign investors, there is strong government support to leverage the plan to advance Brazilian technology. This includes favorable BNDES financing for acquisition of telecom equipment that utilizes Brazilian technology, tax exemptions on the purchase of IT equipment that uses Brazilian technology, as well as favoring national technology in the procurement process. Nonetheless, foreign firms have already begin to participate in the National Broadband plan. To promote Brazilian industry, the Special Agency for Industrial Financing (FINAME) of BNDES provides financing for Brazilian firms to purchase Brazilian-made machinery and equipment and capital goods with a high level of domestic content. The interest rates charged by BNDES are often lower than the prevailing market interest rates for domestic financing.

Brazil is not a signatory to the WTO Agreement on Government Procurement (GPA), and transparency in Brazil's procurement processes is at times lacking. U.S. companies have found it difficult to participate in Brazil's public sector procurement unless they have operations in

Brazil or are associated with a local firm. Without a significant in-country presence, U.S. companies regularly face significant obstacles in winning government contracts and are often more successful in earning subcontracting arrangements with larger Brazilian firms that won the original government bid. Law 8666 (1993) covers most government procurement other than information technology/telecommunications and requires non-discriminatory treatment for all bidders regardless of nationality or origin of the product or service. Brazilian government procurement rules apply to purchases by government entities and state-owned companies. Brazil has an open competition process for major government procurements. By law, the Brazilian government may not make a distinction between domestic and foreign-owned companies during the tendering process; however, when two equally qualified vendors are considered, the law's implementing regulations provide for a preference to Brazilian goods and services. Under Brazilian law, price is to be the overriding factor in selecting suppliers. However, the law's implementing regulations also allow for the consideration of non-price factors, giving preferences to certain goods produced in Brazil and stipulating local content requirements for fiscal benefits eligibility. Additionally, nearly all bids require establishment of a local representative for any foreign company bidding.

A law approved in late 2010 (12,349, December 15, 2010) allows preferences of up to 25 percent in government contracts for products and services made in Brazil, whether by Brazilian or foreign companies. Decree 7174 (2010), which regulates the procurement of information technology goods and services, requires federal agencies and parastatal entities to give preferential treatment to locally produced computer products and goods or services with technology developed in Brazil based on a complicated and nontransparent price/technology matrix. However, Brazil permits foreign companies that have established legal entities in Brazil to compete for procurement-related contracts funded by multilateral development bank loans.

Brazil has a system in place for mortgage registration, but implementation is uneven and there is no standardized contract. Foreign individuals or foreign-owned companies can purchase real property in Brazil. These buyers frequently arrange alternative financing in their own countries, where rates may be more attractive. Law 9514 (1997) helped spur the mortgage industry by establishing a legal framework for a secondary market in mortgages and streamlining the foreclosure process, but the mortgage market in Brazil is still underdeveloped, and foreigners may have difficulty obtaining mortgage financing. Large U.S. real estate firms, nonetheless, are expanding their portfolios in Brazil.

Intellectual Property Rights

Brazil is a signatory to the GATT Uruguay Round Accords, including the Trade Related Aspects of Intellectual Property (TRIPs) Agreement, signed in April 1994. Brazil is a signatory of the Bern Convention on Artistic Property, the Patent Cooperation Treaty, the Convention on Plant Variety Protection, and the

Paris Convention on Protection of Intellectual Property.

Brazil is not a party to the WIPO Copyright Treaty or the WIPO Performances and Phonograms Treaty (collectively, the "WIPO Internet Treaties"). In 2006, Brazil announced plans to join the Madrid Agreement Concerning the International Registration of Marks ("Madrid Protocol"), but the executive branch has yet to submit this proposal to the Brazilian Congress for approval. In most respects, Brazil's 1996 Industrial Property Law (Law 9279) meets the international standards specified in the TRIPs Agreement regarding patent and trademark protection. However, the law permits the grant of a compulsory license if a patent owner has failed to locally manufacture the patented invention in Brazil within three years of patent issuance, a form of compulsory licensing that the United States believes would be inconsistent with Articles 27.1 and 28.1 of TRIPs. On May 4, 2007, invoking TRIPS provisions for public health emergencies, Brazil issued a compulsory license for an anti-retroviral drug used in treating HIV/AIDS. The

United States continues to raise concerns regarding article 229-C of law 9279, as amended by Law 10196 (2001), which includes a requirement for National Health Surveillance Agency (ANVISA) approval prior to the issuance of a pharmaceutical patent by the National Industrial Property Institute (INPI). ANVISA's role in reviewing pharmaceutical patent applications remains non-transparent and has contributed to an increasing backlog in the issuance of patents. In addition, conflicting opinions on patentability between INPI and ANVISA has left 145 patent applications unissued. On October 16, 2009, the Brazilian Federal Attorney General (AGU) analyzing the institutional role of ANVISA in the patent application process, presented Opinion No. 210 stating that ANVISA should examine pharmaceutical patent applications only from a public health perspective. The opinion states that INPI is the only agency with the competency to review the patentability requirements of such applications. On January 10, 2011, the AGU issued a final ruling noting ANVISA's limited role: "ANVISA may not refuse the granting of the prior consent of art. 229-C of IP Law based on patentability requirements." An ongoing concern is the backlog of pending patent applications at INPI. It currently takes an average of eight years to receive a patent in Brazil. However, INPI has increased its hiring and training of new patent examiners in an effort to decrease pendency. In 2011, INPI is looking to begin rolling out an electronic filing system for new patent applications, which would enable inventors to apply for a patent via an online system.

The United States has also raised concerns regarding Brazil's protection against unfair commercial use of test data generated in connection with obtaining marketing approval for human-use pharmaceutical products. Law 10603 (2002) covers data confidentiality for veterinary pharmaceuticals, fertilizers, agro-toxins, and related products, but does not cover pharmaceuticals for human use. A government-drafted bill to provide protection for the layout design of integrated circuits (computer mask works) was enacted into law on May 31, 2007 (Law 11.484). Patent and trademark licensing agreements must be recorded with and approved by INPI and registered with the Central Bank of Brazil (Normative Act No. 135, of April 15, 1997). Licensing contracts must contain detailed information about the terms of the agreement and royalties to be paid. In such arrangements, Brazilian law limits the amount of the royalty payment that can be taken as a tax deduction (from one percent to five percent), which consequently acts as a de facto cap on licensing fees (Act No. 436 of 1958). Brazil's 1998 copyright law generally conform to international standards, yet piracy of copyrighted material remains a problem. The Brazilian Congress passed a law in July 2003 increasing minimum prison sentences for copyright violations and establishing procedures for making arrests and the destruction of confiscated products. However, the heftier sentences have not acted as effective deterrents due to the frequency with which judges commute many of the prison terms to fines. Draft Law 333 of 1999 would stiffen the criminal penalties for counterfeiting, but remains stalled in the Brazilian Congress. After being shelved in 2006, the draft law was re-submitted in November 2008 for urgent reconsideration, but the proposal has not come to a vote. In August 2007, a bill (PL 1807/07) was introduced that, if approved, would amend Article 189 of Brazil's Industrial Property Law (Law 9279 of 1996) to increase the criminal penalties for trademark violations to two to six years, up from the current three to twelve months. The bill has been under consideration in a Brazilian Chamber committee since August 2007.

In the U.S. Trade Representative's 2007 Special 301 Report, Brazil was downgraded from "Priority Watch List" to "Watch List," in recognition of its improved anti-piracy enforcement efforts. Since then, Brazil has remained on the "Watch List" of the Special 301 Reports.

Transparency of the Regulatory System

In the 2011 World Bank "Doing Business" report, Brazil ranked 127th out of 183 countries in terms of overall ease of doing business. According to the study, it takes an average of 15 procedures and 120 days to start a new business. The study noted that the annual administrative burden to a medium-size business of tax payments in Brazil is an average of 2,600 hours versus 199 hours in the OECD high-income economies. According to this same study, the total tax rate for Brazil's medium-sized business is 69.0 percent of profits, compared to 43.0 percent in the OECD high-income economies. Business managers often complain of not understanding tax regulations, despite best efforts including large tax and accounting departments. Tax regulations, while burdensome and numerous, do not differentiate between foreign and domestic firms. However, there have been instances of complaints that the value- added tax collected by individual states (ICMS) favors local companies. Although the tax is designed to be refunded upon export of goods outside of the country, exporters in many states have had difficulty receiving their ICMS rebates. Taxes on commercial and financial transactions are particularly burdensome, and businesses complain that these taxes hinder the international competitiveness of Brazilian products. A government proposal to streamline the tax collection system is currently under consideration by the Brazilian Congress, but remains stalled.

ANVISA, the Brazilian FDA equivalent, has regulatory authority over the production and marketing of food, drugs and medical devices. ANATEL, the country's telecommunication agency, handles licensing and assigns bandwidth. ANP, the National Petroleum Agency, has been commended by the industry. The civil aviation regulator (ANAC) began functioning in 2006 with a mandate to increase competition within Brazil's civil aviation industry. Taking over responsibilities that had previously resided with the Brazilian Air Force, ANAC has begun to take steps to liberalize the Brazilian market, although court challenges have slowed some proposed initiatives such as price liberalization that was intended to be phased in over 2009. Foreign investors have encountered obstacles when interfacing with regulatory agencies. Notable examples include companies in the electric power sector that have complained about the high level of regulatory risk, including the tariff review process. Additionally, some industries have reported challenges in obtaining licenses from IBAMA, the environmental regulator, citing unpredictability in IBAMA's licensing requirements, though the process has reportedly become more streamlined since 2008.

Brazilian private sector organizations, which often include foreign companies, are vocal and involved in industry standards setting. A bill (PL 3937/04) to modernize Brazil's antitrust review and to combine the antitrust functions of the Ministry of Justice and the Ministry of Finance (MoF) into those of the Administrative Council for Economic Defense (CADE) was approved by the Chamber of Deputies in December 2008. The bill, which would also revise the country's licensing and anti-cartel system, is has been amended by the senate and currently awaits review in the chamber.

Recent Changes and Concerns in Legislation Regulating Business Operations In 2010, Brazil's Congress approved and then-President Lula signed a series of laws that will govern development of the promising deep water "pre-salt" oil and gas reserves found off Brazil's coast. (President Lula vetoed, however, portions of the legislation that would address division of royalties between state and municipal governments.) The new regime replaces Brazil's former concessions model for exploration and production of pre- salt reserves with a production sharing system. The legislation creates a new government entity to represent the government in any agreements, gives sole operator status and a minimum 30 percent stake to the parastatal oil company Petrobras for any pre-salt project, and establishes a social fund to administer the government's proceeds. A law also enabled the government to engage in an oil-for-shares swap with Petrobras, which not only increased government ownership in the parastatal, but also facilitated Petrobras' USD 67 billion public share offering in September 2010.

Reinsurance industry representatives have expressed concern over regulatory changes that took effect in early 2011. The changes prohibit insurers from placing more than 20% of their reinsurance business with reinsurers with which they are affiliated and require 40 percent of reinsurance business to be placed with Brazilian reinsurers. In October 2010, the Brazilian tax and customs authority, Receita Federal, launched a new automated system for express delivery customs processing. The new Sistema Remessa will allow for paper-free electronic clearance for express delivery goods. This is an important first step, but companies continue to express concern over remaining regulatory challenges that they face, including high import taxes, low maximum value limits for express export and import shipments and the possible approval of a damaging postal reform law that could undermine current levels of market access for private express delivery service companies.

Efficient Capital Markets and Portfolio Investment

The Brazilian financial sector is large and sophisticated. Banks lend at the Brazilian market rate which remains extremely high. Reasons cited by industry observers include high taxation, repayment risk, concern over inconsistent judicial enforcement of contracts, high mandatory reserve requirements, and administrative overhead. The financial sector is concentrated, with 2010 Central Bank data indicating that the 10 largest commercial banking institutions account for approximately

72.9 percent of financial sector assets, less brokerages (approx. USD 1.69 trillion). Two of the five largest banks (in assets) in the country, Banco do Brasil and Caixa Economica Federal, are federally owned. Lending by the large banking institutions is focused on the largest companies, while small and medium banks primarily serve small and medium-sized companies, but with a much smaller capital base.

The Central Bank has strengthened bank audits, implemented more stringent internal control requirements, and tightened capital adequacy rules to better reflect risk. It also established loan classification and provisioning requirements. These measures are applied to private and publicly owned banks alike. The Brazilian Securities Exchange Commission (CVM) independently regulates the stock exchanges, brokers, distributors, pension funds, mutual funds, and leasing companies with penalties against insider trading.

Credit Market

Brazil's credit market has grown significantly over the past several years. Real (after inflation) interest rates, however, remain among the highest in the world, leading large enterprises operating in Brazil to access financing on international markets. While local private sector banks are beginning to offer longer credit terms, BNDES, the government national development bank, is the traditional Brazilian source of longer-term credit, and also provides export credits. FINAME (the Special Agency for Industrial Financing) provides foreign and domestically owned companies operating in Brazil financing for the manufacturing and marketing of capital goods. FINAMEX (Export Financing), which finances capital good exports for both foreign and domestic companies, is a part of FINAME. One of the goals of these financing options is to support the purchase of domestic over imported equipment and machinery. PROEX, an export credit program financed by the National Treasury offers assistance in the areas of interest rate equalization, capital and other goods exports, and service exports. (See OPIC and Other Investment Insurance Programs section for more information on credit availability).

Equity Market

All stock trading is performed on the Sao Paulo Stock Exchange (BOVESPA), while trading of public securities is conducted on the Rio de Janeiro market. In 2008, the Brazilian Mercantile & Futures Exchange (BM&F) merged with the BOVESPA to form what is now the fourth largest exchange in the Western Hemisphere, after the NYSE, NASDAQ, and Canadian TSX Group exchanges. BOVESPA has launched a "New Market," in which the listed companies comply with stricter corporate governance requirements. In June 2004, BOVESPA's new market had 18 listed companies; by 2010 there were 112. (Note: A majority of the Initial Public Offerings are listed on the New Market). In 2010, there were twenty-two new IPOs and follow-ons representing R$ 39.4 billion in raised capital; approximately 27 percent of this amount was foreign capital. After a decline in 2009, the total number of companies listed on the BOVESPA resumed its course of growth in 2010. There were 394 companies in 2006, 424 in 2008, 386 in 2009, and 471 in 2010. Total daily trading average volume has risen from R$ 2.4 billion in 2006 to R$ 6.5 billion in 2010.

Trading is highly concentrated, with the top ten stocks accounting for nearly half of the 2010 trading volume. A total of 80 Brazilian firms are also listed on the NYSE via American Depository Receipts (ADR's). Conversely, the Brazilian subsidiaries of some U.S. companies have issued shares on the BOVESPA.

Foreign investors, both institutions and individuals, can directly invest in equities, securities and derivatives. Foreign investors are required to trade derivatives and stocks of publicly held companies on established markets. At year-end 2010, foreign investors accounted for 29.6 percent of the total turnover on the BOVESPA. Domestic institutional investors were the most active market participants, accounting for 33.3 percent of activity. Individual investors comprised 26.4 of activity, financial institutions 8.4, and other companies 2.3 percent. Since 2001, Law 10303 has limited preferred shares for new issuances to 50 percent.

Brazilian law recognizes mergers and consolidations. Although the stock market is growing in popularity, sales of Brazilian companies usually result from private negotiations, rather than stock exchange activities. Acquisitions resulting in market concentration in excess of 20 percent are subject to review by the Administrative Council for Economic Defense (CADE) under Brazil's 1994 Anti-trust Law. Wholly owned subsidiaries of multinational accounting firms, including the major U.S. firms, are present in Brazil. As of 1996, auditors are personally liable for the accuracy of accounting statements prepared for banks. In recent years the government has sought to control appreciation of the Brazilian currency with the introduction of new taxes on capital inflows (see "Conversion and Transfer Policies" section above).

Competition from State Owned Enterprises

Since the early 1990's, the Brazilian government has aggressively privatized state enterprises across a broad spectrum of industries, including mining, steel, aeronautics, banking, energy, and electricity generation and distribution. While the government has divested itself from many of its state-owned companies, it maintains partial control (at both the federal and state level) of previously wholly state-owned enterprises. Notable examples of partially federally-controlled firms include energy giant Petrobras and power utility Eletrobras. Both Petrobras and Eletrobras include non-government shareholders, are listed on both the Brazilian and NYSE stock exchanges, and are subject to the same accounting and audit regulations as all publicly traded Brazilian companies. In addition to major players like Petrobras and Eletrobras, the Brazilian government, at both the federal and state levels, maintains ownership interests in a variety of other smaller enterprises. Typically, corporate governance is led by a board comprised of directors elected by the state or federal government with additional directors elected by the other non-government shareholders. Brazilian enterprises with state ownership are concentrated in the energy, electricity generation and distribution, transportation, and banking sectors. Many of these firms are also publically traded companies on the Brazilian and other stock exchanges.

The 2010 pre-salt legislation, described above in "Recent Changes and Concerns in Legislation Regulating Business Operations" gives the parastatal oil company Petrobras sole operator status for the development of the new oil discoveries. The terms and conditions of the new regime may favor Petrobras as the sole operator, although foreign firms are still anticipated to play a role in the pre-salt oil fields. In December of 2008, the Brazilian Ministry of Finance established a sovereign wealth fund (SWF) with initial capital of R$14.2 billion financed through a government bond issuance. Brazil's SWF is managed by the Fiscal Investment and Stabilization Fund (FFIE), a vehicle established for the sole purpose of managing the fund. The FFIE is structured similarly to any other financial fund manager in Brazil and subject to the same regulatory and transparency guidelines, including external and independent auditing. The SWF was designed to be an anti-cyclical tool to help absorb the impacts of financial downturns. There are no material restrictions on how the SWF can be used, apart from the fact that it must maintain a tolerable risk profile. Currently the SWF is entirely domestically focused, but it is authorized to invest outside of Brazil. In 2010, the government confirmed that the SWF was authorized to buy U.S. dollars, including in the futures market, creating a new tool for the government to intervene in foreign exchange markets to curb the appreciation of the Brazilian currency. Detailed public information relating to the SWF is available on a Ministry of Finance website, and the Brazilian Congress receives regular performance reports.

Corporate Social Responsibility

Most state-owned and private sector corporations of any significant size in Brazil pursue corporate social responsibility (CSR) activities. Many corporations support local education, health and other programs in the communities where they have a presence. Brazilian consumers, especially the local citizenry where a corporation has or is planning a local presence, expect CSR activity. It is not uncommon that corporate officials will meet with community members prior to building a new plant or factory to review what types of local services the corporation will commit to providing. Foreign and local enterprises in Brazil often advance United Nations Development Program (UNDP) Millennium Development Goals (MDGs) as part of their CSR activity, and will cite their local contributions to MDGs such as universal primary education and environmental sustainability. The U.S. Diplomatic Mission in Brazil supports American business CSR activities through the +Unidos Group (Mais Unidos), a group of more than 100 American companies established in Brazilian territory.

Political Violence

Political and labor strikes and demonstrations occur occasionally in urban areas and may cause temporary disruption to public transportation. In addition, criminal organizations in Sao Paulo have in the past staged campaigns against public institutions. While U.S. citizens have not been targeted during such events, U.S. citizens traveling or residing in Brazil are advised to take commonsense precautions and avoid any large gatherings or any other event where crowds have congregated to demonstrate or protest.

Colombian terrorist groups have been known to operate in the border areas of neighboring countries. Colombian groups have perpetrated kidnappings of residents and tourists in border areas of Colombia's neighbors. The U.S. Government knows of no specific threat directed against U.S. citizens across the border in Brazil at this time. U.S. citizens traveling or residing in areas of Brazil near the Colombian border are urged to exercise caution. U.S. citizens are urged to take care when visiting remote parts of the Amazon basin and respect local laws and customs.

Corruption

Corruption can be a challenge to some kinds of investment in Brazil. In 2010, Brazil ranked 69th (among 178 countries) in Transparency International's Corruption Perception Index. In South America, Brazil ranked below Chile and Uruguay, and ranked above Colombia, Peru, Argentina and Venezuela. With regard to major emerging economies, Brazil ranked above India, China, Russia, Egypt, and Indonesia, and below South Africa and Turkey. In general terms, press reports and companies suggest corruption is a challenge in government procurement and at some levels of the judiciary.

Many corruption investigations, involving politicians from both opposition and government coalition parties, have been conducted over the course of the last several years. In 2010, in two separate cases, the governor of the Federal District and the governor of the state of Amapa were arrested and placed in prison on corruption charges. Brazil's anti-money laundering mechanisms and relatively independent prosecutorial and oversight institutions have played useful roles in the investigation of such cases. In June of 2010, the President signed into law Complementary Law 135, known as the "Ficha Limpa" law, which prohibits candidates convicted of crimes, including abuse of public office, from running for office. The Brazilian Supreme Court subsequently implemented the Ficha Limpa with respect to the 2010 federal, state, and local elections although later court decisions modified its implementation. Brazil is a signatory to the Organization for Economic Cooperation and Development (OECD) Anti-Bribery Convention. Brazil has laws, regulations and penalties to combat corruption, but their effectiveness is inconsistent. Bribery is illegal, and a bribe by a local company to a foreign official is a criminal act. A company cannot deduct a bribe to a foreign official from its taxes. While federal government authorities generally investigate allegations of corruption, there are inconsistencies in the level of enforcement among individual states. Press reports and companies indicate that corruption remains problematic in business dealings with some parts of the Brazilian government, particularly on the local level. U.S. companies operating in Brazil continue to be subject to the U.S. Foreign Corrupt Practices Act.

Bilateral Investment Agreements

Brazil does not have a Bilateral Investment Treaty with the United States. While in the 1990's Brazil signed BITs with Belgium and Luxembourg, Chile, Cuba, Denmark, Finland,

France, Germany, Italy, Republic of Korea, Netherlands, Portugal, Switzerland, United Kingdom and Venezuela, none of these have been approved by the Brazilian Congress. Brazil also has not approved the Mercosul investment protocol. Brazil has no double taxation treaty with the United States, but it does have such treaties with 24 other countries, including, among others, Japan, France, Italy, the Netherlands, Canada and Argentina. Brazil signed a Tax Information Exchange Agreement with the United States in March 2007 that passed the Brazilian chamber in December 2009 and currently awaits action in the Brazilian Senate.

Labor

The 92.7 million strong Brazilian labor force comprises a wide range of skills covering a broad array of occupations and industries. Slightly more than three fifths, or 61 percent, of the labor force is employed in the service sector, 17 percent in the agriculture sector, and the civil construction and manufacturing sectors combined employ the remaining 22 percent. Brazil has signed on to a large number of

International Labor Organization (ILO) conventions. Brazil is party to the U.N. Convention on the Rights of the Child and major ILO conventions concerning the prohibition of child labor, forced labor and discrimination. The labor code is highly detailed and relatively generous to workers.

Formal sector workers are guaranteed 30 days of annual leave, an annual bonus equal to one month's salary, and severance pay in the case of dismissal without cause. Brazil also has a system of labor courts that are charged with resolving routine cases involving unfair dismissal, working conditions, salary disputes, and other grievances. Labor courts have the power to impose an agreement on employers and unions if negotiations break down and either side appeals to the court system. As a result, labor courts routinely are called upon to determine wages and working conditions in industries across the country. The system is tantamount to compulsory arbitration and does not encourage collective bargaining. In recent years, however, both labor and management have become more flexible and collective bargaining has assumed greater relevance. The Ministry of Labor estimates that there are over 16,000 labor unions in Brazil, but Ministry officials note that these figures are inexact. Labor unions, especially in sectors such as metalworking and banking, tend to be well-organized and aggressive in defending wages and working conditions and account for approximately 19 percent of the official workforce according to the last Brazilian Institute of Geography and Statistics (IBGE) release (2005). Strikes occur periodically, particularly among public sector unions. Unions in various sectors engage in industry-wide collective bargaining negotiations mandated by federal regulation. While some labor organizations and their leadership operate independently of the government and of political parties, others are viewed as closely associated with political parties.

In firms employing three or more persons, Brazilian nationals must constitute at least two-thirds of all employees and receive at least two-thirds of total payroll. Foreign specialists in fields where Brazilians are unavailable are not counted in calculating the one-third permitted for non-Brazilians. The IBGE estimated unemployment in the major metropolitan areas as of November 2010 at 6.1 percent (versus 7.4 percent in November 2009). With low unemployment, there is currently a shortage of highly-skilled workers. Unemployment levels range significantly across regions. IBGE reports show that real wages have trended higher in recent years. The average monthly wage in Brazil's six largest cities was around 1,516 Reais in November 2010 (approximately USD 892 based on average exchange rates for that month). The minimum monthly wage has regularly been increased in recent years from 380 Reais in 2007 to the 545 Reais that the government announced in January 2011. Earnings vary significantly by region and industry, and there is significant income inequality between Brazil's poor and wealthy. Employer federations, supported by mandatory fees based on payroll, play a significant role in both public policy and labor relations. Each state has its own federation, which reports to CNI (National Confederation of Industries), headquartered in Brasilia.

Foreign Trade Zones

The federal government has granted tax benefits for certain free trade zones. The most prominent of these is the Manaus Free Trade Zone, in Amazonas State, which has attracted significant foreign investment, including from U.S. companies. The GOB estimated 2010 revenues generated in the Manaus industrial area to have reached approximately USD 30 billion. Most of these free trade zones aim to attract investment to the country's relatively underdeveloped North and Northeast regions.

Foreign Direct Investment

According to the Central Bank's most recent foreign-capital census (2005), the United States and the Netherlands had the largest share of accumulated foreign-capital stock in Brazil, each with 16.6 percent of the total. Spain had 10.8 percent, Mexico 10.7 percent, and France 7.5 percent. Investment inflows between the years 2006 to 2009 have amounted to about USD 130 billion, exclusive of depreciation and capital repatriation. The Central Bank expects to publish an updated foreign capital stock report in 2011. According to a Brazilian Central Bank market survey report, FDI inflows to Brazil are anticipated to have reached USD 33.0 billion in 2010. According to the U.S. Bureau of Economic Analysis, FDI inflows from the United States to Brazil were USD 2.7 billion in 2009 and the stock of FDI from the United States to Brazil was USD 56.7 billion as of the end of 2009.

Chapter 5: Trade and Project Financing

How Do I Get Paid (Methods of Payment)

Imports in Brazil are primarily handled using traditional letters of credit (L/C) or collections through established banks with correspondent banking agreements overseas. To a lesser extent, U.S. exporters may choose to operate on an open account or cash in advance basis once they have established a trustworthy relationship with their Brazilian buyers. (Note: given high interest rates and intermediary spreads, Brazilian buyers are likely to push for open account or cash up front. We highly recommend that U.S. companies work with Ex-Im Bank insurance or guarantees to ensure payment).

Credit & Collection

Credit information on Brazilian companies is available for a fee from Dun & Bradstreet (http://www.dnb.com.br), Equifax (http://www.equifax.com.br) or SERASA, a

Brazilian commercial information service company (http://www.serasa.com.br). In the event of a commercial dispute or non-payment by a Brazilian importer requiring legal action, the U.S. exporter should contact a renowned legal firm with experience in international collections. Local collection agencies do not handle international disputes. The U.S. Commercial Service in Brazil can furnish lists of law firms through our Customized Contact List (CCL) or International Partner Search (IPS). We can also set up meetings with them through our Gold Key Service (GKS).

How Does the Banking System Operate

The Brazilian banking system today is extremely efficient. Most banks have sophisticated Internet sites offering most, if not all, of their products and services. Bank branches are numerous and nearly all cities in the country have at least one major bank branch. The top five banks have approximately 15,000 branches throughout Brazil. International operations are centralized at the bank's headquarters, usually in São Paulo or Rio de Janeiro, although major branches at larger cities may handle routine operations involving trade finance. All Brazilian banks have a number of correspondent banks around the world. Number of foreign banks and origin.

Foreign-Exchange Controls

In Brazil, accounts can only be kept in local currency (Brazilian reais, R$). For a Brazilian importer to remit funds to a seller in the United States, the importer must purchase the corresponding foreign funds by means of an exchange contract at any bank authorized by the Brazilian Central Bank. The exchange rate and related fees are negotiated directly between the purchaser of the foreign currency (the importer) and the bank.

The Brazilian Central Bank is a federal agency entrusted to implement the federal government National Monetary Council's (Conselho Monetario Nacional) policies to improve and stabilize the national financial system. Its functions include the control of foreign capital flows.

U.S. Banks and Local Correspondent Banks

Following the acquisition of BankBoston by Banco Itau in May 2006, the U.S. presence in the Brazilian banking system was reduced to regular commercial bank activities by Citibank, investment banking by JP Morgan and Morgan Stanley, and consumer credit for automobile purchases by General Motors (Banco GMAC).

Brazil's strong foreign trade sector and increasing trade activities have led the large banks to increase the number of correspondent banks around the globe, in new and expanding markets as well as with traditional trade partners such as the United States. Note: the U.S. Export Import Bank (Ex-Im) provides both export insurance and working capital for U.S. exporters and guaranteed loans for Brazilian importers. Local companies can arrange at-market or even below-market direct loans with the Brazilian National Economic Development Bank (BNDES). In many cases, the funds can be used to purchase goods from U.S. exporters. Some companies claim that the loan approval process is bureaucratic and consequently slow.

Import Finance by a Latin American Bank (in Foreign Currency):

A Latin American bank pays a U.S. exporter in advance for goods to be shipped to a Latin American buyer. The Latin American bank is essentially providing the buyer a loan and the buyer will have to repay the bank per their financing agreement. In Latin America, this type of financing generally has a six-month grace period after which the buyer must begin repaying the Bank. Although this option is extremely expensive for Latin American buyers, it is frequently the only alternative available to them, particularly when they are purchasing larger ticket capital equipment items. Ex-Im also offers a variety of trade and project finance options.

Chapter 6: Business Travel

Business Customs

Business visitors should be aware of several business conditions specific to Brazil. Compared to the United States, the pace of negotiations is slower and is heavily based on personal contact. It is rare for important business deals to be concluded by telephone or letter. Many Brazilian executives do not react favorably to quick and infrequent visits by foreign sales representatives, or to changes in the negotiating team. They prefer a more continuous working relationship. The Brazilian buyer is also concerned with after- sales service provided by the exporter.

The Brazilian approach to time is somewhat flexible, with scheduled meetings often starting late and/or running later than expected. Prepare your agenda in order to accommodate these possible changes. Persistent traffic issues, especially in São Paulo, means that sufficient time should be scheduled for transportation as well. It is advisable to be punctual, and to not show signs of frustration or impatience with delays. During a first visit to a company it is customary to give a gift, usually promotional items without great material value. Expensive gifts can be misunderstood as bribes and are not welcome. Be aware that business dress is often formal and conservative, in spite of the apparent informality while conducting business.

Personal space standards in Brazil are different than those in the United States. It is not uncommon for a local contact to stand very close while speaking, pat a business contact on the shoulder or even hug that person. In spite of the difference in personal space, it is better to act more formal rather than less during an initial meeting. Also, communication in Brazil happens in an overlapped manner, with people interrupting each other constantly – that is a sign of interest on the subject, not of disrespect.

Logistics

A passport and visa are required for U.S. citizens traveling to Brazil for any purpose. There are no "airport visas," and immigration authorities will refuse entry to Brazil to anyone not possessing a valid visa. All Brazilian visas, regardless of the length of validity, must initially be used within 90 days of the issuance date or will no longer be valid. The U.S. Government cannot assist travelers who arrive in Brazil without proper documentation.

Minors (under 18) traveling alone, with one parent or with a third party, must present written authorization by the absent parent(s) or legal guardian specifically granting permission to travel alone, with one parent, or with a third party. The authorization (in Portuguese) must be notarized and then authenticated by the Brazilian Embassy or Consulate.

Telecommunications standards in Brazil are good. Internet can easily be found in major hotels as well as Internet cafes. Within metropolitan areas the phone system is reliable and most people use cell phones. Brazil has numerous international and domestic airports. The country's size will likely require U.S. business people to fly domestically within Brazil. The country's taxi services run very well, though U.S. citizens are recommended to not simply hail them on the street but rather meet one at a taxi stand or ask the restaurant, hotel or other establishment to call one. Public transportation is available, though in major metropolitan areas it can often be unsafe.

Portuguese is Brazil's official language. English proficiency varies among Brazilian business persons. It is usually a good idea to have a translator accompany you on meetings and business calls. Correspondence and product literature should be in Portuguese, and English is preferred as a substitute over Spanish. Specifications and other technical data should be in the metric system.

Health

Crime rates throughout Brazil are high, especially in large cities. The incidence of crime against tourists is greater in areas surrounding beaches, hotels, discotheques, bars, nightclubs, and other similar establishments that cater to visitors and is especially prevalent during Carnaval (Brazilian Mardi Gras). Occasionally, crime against tourists has been violent and has led to some deaths. While the risk is greater at dusk and during evening hours, street crime can occur any time and areas considered "safer" are not immune. Incidents of theft on city buses are frequent, and such transportation should be avoided. Several Brazilian cities have established specialized tourist police units to patrol areas frequented by tourists.

"Express kidnappings," where victims are abducted and forced to withdraw money from ATMs, occur often enough to warrant caution. At airports, hotel lobbies, bus stations and other public places there is much pick-pocketing, and the theft of carry-on luggage, briefcases, and laptop computers is common (including some reports of thefts on internal flights). Travelers should "dress down" when outside and avoid carrying valuables or wearing jewelry or expensive watches. "Good Samaritan" scams are common. If a tourist looks lost or seems to be having trouble communicating, they may be victimized by a seemingly innocent and helpful bystander. Care should be taken at and around banks and internationally connected automatic teller machines that take U.S. credit or debit cards. Poor neighborhoods known as "favelas" are found throughout Brazil. These areas are sites of criminal activity and are often not patrolled by police. U.S. citizens are advised to avoid these unsafe areas.

While the ability of Brazilian police to help recover stolen property is limited, it is nevertheless strongly advised to obtain a "boletim de ocorrencia" (police report) at a "delegacia" (police station) whenever any possessions are lost or stolen. This will facilitate the traveler's exit from Brazil and insurance claims.

Yellow fever vaccination is recommended if the travelers' destination in Brazil includes any of the following States: Acre, Amazonas, Amapá, Federal District (Brasilia), Goiás, Maranhão, Mato Grosso, Mato Grosso do Sul, Pará, Rondônia, Roraima and Tocantins. A polio vaccination certificate is mandatory at the port of entry in Brazil for children between the ages of 3 months and 6 years.

Brazil observes daylight savings from October to February. When daylight savings is in effect in the United States, i.e. March to November,

Brazilian time is one hour ahead of Eastern Daylight Time. When daylight savings is in effect in Brazil, i.e. October to February, Brazilian time is three hours ahead of Eastern Standard Time. While office hours in Brazil are generally 8 am - 6 pm, decision-makers begin work later in the morning and stay later in the evening. The best times for calls on a Brazilian executive are between 10 am - noon, and 3 - 5 pm, although this is less the case for São Paulo where appointments are common throughout most of the day. Lunch often lasts two hours.

Chapter 7: Contacts

U.S. Commercial Service Brazil

Deputy Senior Commercial Officer: Scott Shaw

(Scott.Shaw@trade.gov)

Phone: 011-55-11-5186-7191;

Fax: 011-55-11-5186-7343

Rua Thomas Deloney,

381 Chacara Santo Antonio 04710-041

São Paulo, SP

U.S. Commercial Service Belo Horizonte

Commercial   Assistant: Robert   Pohl

(Robert.Pohl@trade.gov)

Ph: 011-55-31-3213-1571;

Fax: 011-55-31-3213-1575

Rua Timbiras,

1200, 7º andar 30140-060

Belo Horizonte, MG

U.S. Commercial Service Brasilia

Principal Commercial Officer. Devin Rambo

(Devin.Rambo@trade.gov)

Ph: 011-55-61-3312-7403;

Fax: 011-55-61-3312-7656

SES - Av. das Nações,

Quadra 801, Lote 0370403-900

Brasilia, DF

U.S. Commercial Service Rio de Janeiro

Principal Commercial Officer: Alan Long

(Alan.Long@trade.gov)

Ph: 011-55-21-3823-2000;

Fax: 011-55-21-3823-2424

Av. Presidente Wilson,

147, 4° Andar 20030-020

Rio de Janeiro, RJ

U.S. Commercial Service Recife

Commercial Specialist: Adierson Azevedo

(Adierson.Azevedo@trade.gov)

Ph: 011-81-3416-3075;

Fax: 011-55-81-3231-1906

Rua Gonçalves Maia,

163 - Boa Vista 50070-060

Recife, PE

U.S. Commercial Service São Paulo

Commercial Officer: Sean Kelley

(Sean.Kelley@trade.gov)

Ph: 011-55-11-5186-7429;

Fax: 011-55-11-5186-7445

Rua Thomas Deloney,

381 Chacara Santo Antonio 04710-041

São Paulo, SP

The Internationalist®

International Business, Investment,

and Travel

www.internationalist.com

www.ingramcontent.com/pod-product-compliance
Lightning Source LLC
Chambersburg PA
CBHW051503170526
45166CB00001B/366